SHOULD THE CHILDREN KNOW?

Encounters with Death in the Lives of Children

MARGUERITA RUDOLPH

SCHOCKEN BOOKS · NEW YORK

First published by SCHOCKEN BOOKS 1978

10 9 8 7 6 5 4 3   80 81 82 83 84

Copyright © 1978 by Schocken Books Inc.

Library of Congress Cataloging in Publication Data

Rudolph, Marguerita.
Should the children know?

1. Children and death.   I. Title.

BF723.D3R83   155.9'37   77-73974

Manufactured in the United States of America

ISBN 0-8052-0662-0

In memory of my mother,
Sofia Samoilovna Beliavskaya,
and my father,
Khaim Yakovlevich Gurvich

CONTENTS

INTRODUCTION

"Why have you chosen such a frightful subject?" I was asked when I started to write this book. Other questions and comments from friends and acquaintances had similar implications. However, in recent months, the predominant reaction of people who had learned of my work-in-progress was: What a good idea—we know *little* about such an important subject!

As parents and teachers, and as relatives and friends of children, we face at one time or another the fact of death. Invariably we face it with difficulty—the difficulty of handling our own emotions, the difficulty of expressing our understanding and of sharing our concern, and especially the difficulty for adults to relate to children on a significant matter.

Children, even very young ones, respond deeply to the people, objects, and events in their surroundings. They respond by feeling, noticing, touching, absorbing. They do it in accordance with their capacity, their experience, and in accordance with the freedom as well as the restrictions in their lives. What they encounter and absorb, what thoughts and feelings are generated, what values might be gained in the process are profoundly interesting to adults living with and caring for children. How children react and what they learn from encounters with death have been of special interest to me.

The material for this book was gathered from my work with children and parents, from studying and reading, and from being a mother and a grandmother. An additional source was my own childhood experience with death. The incidents in the book are all true, including those quoted from my previous publications; they have been taken from records and altered for literary purposes.

SHOULD THE
CHILDREN KNOW?

1

"TELL THEM RACHEL MOVED"

summarize this story

Parents of young children attending a child-care center, a nursery school, or a kindergarten are often surprised at how intimately involved the teacher is with the children; how familiar with their physical well-being and maturity; how aware of their feelings (or even their quirks). Such involvement not only supports the educational process, but expresses also the teacher's humanness and her relationship with the children. And such involvement with young children necessarily includes meaningful, ongoing communication with parents.

When a significant project is undertaken in her class, an important event is about to take place, or unexpected trouble occurs (all of which have a serious effect on both teacher and children), the teacher has a will and a way to share her own and the children's concerns with parents, and a desire to reach out for understanding from them.

As a nursery-school teacher, I acted on my feelings and judgment to summon urgently all the parents of the twenty children in my class—all but one couple, the parents of four-and-a-half-year-old Rachel. Rachel had died at home that day.

As this happened in the spring, I knew the children intimately and cared about each one. Naturally, Rachel's death was a blow that caused me profound sorrow and a sense of inexpressible loss. At the same time I knew that Rachel's absence would be noticed by the children and her death would be surmised, even if nothing were said to them. And if they were told, the news would be likely to produce sadness, fear, confusion, possible trauma, or some delayed strange behavior among them. I was deeply concerned with my responsibility to them as a teacher.

As a teacher, what should I convey to them? How? I did not think that a book or persons in authority could provide *the* answer. I needed to search for an answer in myself first. What seemed important to me was to learn now from this particular life experience. What I needed to carry out my responsibility as a teacher was to learn from the parents how they intended to communicate to the children the news of Rachel's death. I wanted to know how they felt about it, and what they believed was appropriate information for a nursery-school child. I wanted also to discuss with them my ideas of teaching at a time of death in the children's midst.

As I had expected they would, all the parents responded to the urgent summons, and all of them came that evening. How different a roomful of adults is from a roomful of children. The parents required a different kind of communication; they presented a different challenge. I hoped they would be free to express their reaction to the tragic happening and share their ideas as to what the children should know about Rachel's death.

When I told them exactly what had happened to Rachel,* several parents wanted to hear what I, the teacher, had to say. Although they needed help in getting such an emotional topic started, I did not, however, offer my opinion first. Instead, I explained that the *parents'* relationship with their children and what the children learn at home is of great importance, and that the teacher's opinion did not constitute total wisdom. To deal intelligently, caringly, with their children on this serious matter, I, the teacher, needed to know where the parents stood, how *they* felt about the subject of death before conveying my special knowledge and arriving at an understanding. I soon sensed that the dominant feeling of the parents was protectiveness toward their children, and a desire to shield them from the knowledge of death.

The flow of speaking out in the group began with a mother saying, "Tell them Rachel moved." And, although no one expressed objection, she nevertheless attempted to justify her statement. "After all, this happens quite often. People move." No parent questioned this; it fitted in with the wish not to have the children learn so early in life of this greatest dread of all. The parents sought an explanation that would be credible to the children. "I think they would accept it if you said Rachel went to visit some relative out of town. Taking a trip is a great thing for a child—it sure is for Peter," one of them offered. Testing the credibility of this, a mother wanted to know, "But wouldn't they *ask* when she's coming back?"

*The medical name of her sudden strange disease is "asphyxiation pneumonia."

"Say 'after school is out,' and by that time they'd forget. Most of them." But there was no expression of conviction either on the part of those who spoke or those who listened. There were only further expressions of a wish to conceal the fact of death from the children.

Though I was myself convinced that concealment of anything important was neither workable nor wise, I was not ready to offer such judgment; I felt reluctant to disturb the parents' comfort in evasion. I waited longer for my confrontation with the painful truth till other parents spoke.

"I have a question, Mrs. Rudolph," a father said. "Can children of four and five years of age *understand* death?"

"No, Mr. N., not in the sense they can understand something they themselves have seen or experienced, but . . ."

"Well, then," Mr. N. hastened to complete his thought, "why worry them with something that's beyond them? Just tell them Rachel has gone somewhere, or moved."

Not only Mr. N. but many others were satisfied with such logic; some were relieved that a difficult problem was actually being solved! It was up to me to draw a conclusion.

"What you'd tell them then is that Rachel is no longer with them, because she has *gone* somewhere—deliberately; and this way you'd keep the knowledge of death from them."

"Yes."

"Yet you would at the same time be *aware* of keeping something from the children . . . I mean *I* would be aware in speaking with the children that I was concealing something important from them, and feel the sadness myself."

There was a look of recognition on the faces of many parents—admission perhaps of similar awareness on their part. They were sympathetic and thoughtful as I continued: "Well, I find that children usually *sense* when you are holding back important news, whether the news is understandable or not, and they 'read' your feelings about it."

"Even children this young?"

"Yes. When the news matters—as Rachel's death matters *to me* because she was in my class and I cared about her, and to the children because she was a member of their group and they knew her."

"But if you don't tell them, and they don't know *what* you are holding back, won't they forget it after a while?" a mother wanted to know.

"Maybe some children would. But some would not stop wondering about the withheld facts, and imagine wildly *what* might have happened that is too terrible to tell. Some children develop complicated worries and lasting fears which take time and special attention to overcome or to outgrow."

A couple of parents concurred that children do feel hidden trouble, but they still wished to escape rather than face the problem. "If only it had happened during the summer—we wouldn't have all this. . . ."

"What's the use of speculating?" another parent replied. "It's happened now. And we have to tell the children."

There were nods and words of agreement to that statement, and I was about to discuss a tentative plan of talking with the children in class—of making the tragic event of Rachel's death known to them—when a determined hand went up from a back seat and an authoritative voice commanded everyone's attention. A clergyman father had something to say. Some of us felt a twinge of guilt because we had passed over religion, and had not sought the clergyman's opinion. The clergyman, Mr. A., spoke directly to the religious point.

"A young child, you must agree, is highly impressionable and receptive. Receptive to what we, the parents and teachers, offer him," Mr. A. said with effective sincerity. "And it is our duty on an occasion of such significance to offer the child our religious belief. This occasion is an opportunity to tell the children that God is in command of what has happened. God is always in command; and Rachel now is in His hands. She is now in heaven."

The implication was that children would accept heaven on faith. They would suffer no worries or fears about either death or heaven. Heaven is certainly something good. What could be better than something "heavenly"? Therefore, Mr. A.'s statement seemed positive, his advice simple. There were expressions of sympathy with the clergyman's view on many faces as well as in the words of members of the group. And I felt obligated and challenged to make a sympathetic reply.

"Yes, religious beliefs about death and heaven can be effectively taught at home. If you, as a family, subscribe to a particular religion and live by it, you share your convictions with your children by example, and you answer their questions according to *your* religious beliefs. In that case, traditional religious interpretations and explanations are a way of family life, with faith and with comfort from unquestioned belief.

"However, the families in our school have different religions, or no official religion. I, therefore, couldn't teach them or indoctrinate them with any aspect of religion. My explanations would have to be in nonreligious terms."

"Then what will you tell the child who asks you in school about heaven?"

"I can say, 'Your mommy or daddy or someone else at home can tell you better what heaven is. I can tell you about other things.' I would not deny a child's belief in heaven. As a matter of fact, the subject of heaven did come up in my class last year. One child insisted on placing our pet turtle on the floor and stepping on it. I rescued the turtle, of course, and asked why he wanted to hurt it. His answer was very plain: 'I want the turtle to die so I can see it go to heaven.'"

The parents were impressed and amused by the anecdote and it brought a bit of levity to the tension in the room.

"But that's a *rare* incident, Mrs. Rudolph," the clergyman father observed.

"True, Mr. A. However, this little boy's exaggerated behavior demonstrates a young child's literal kind of thinking. When he hears that to die is to go to heaven, he thinks that *going* to heaven must be like *going* to the store (rather fun), and he wants to *see* the trip."

"So what did you say to *him* about heaven?"

"I had to be practical and honest for the sake of the other children who gathered on the scene and for the sake of the turtle (who was about to be sacrificed), as well as for the child's sake. To me, the problem was not religious. I said, 'I will not let you hurt the turtle.' I wanted to tell Frankie and the other children only what they could understand, and said: 'You can *see* what the turtle can *do*—climb and swim. But when you hurt it and the turtle dies it can't do anything.' And when he still wanted to see 'heaven' I gave him a literal answer, without making fun of him: 'No heaven in this room.'"

This school account was interesting to the parents, but not something which they thought likely to happen at home. There were further questions.

"It seems to me you are bringing in another problem. When the children are taught one thing at home and something different at school, whom can they believe?"

"I see what you mean. This may well be confusing for a while. But children learn to recognize the difference between home and school. They absorb different knowledge from each, and are not necessarily the worse for it."

Coming back to the main subject of the meeting, I asked the parents if they objected to or questioned my intention to tell the children during class that Rachel had died, without making direct reference to God or heaven, but accepting any child's religious belief, if it were expressed. I told them of my own feeling of sadness and my wish to share it with the children, rather than pretending to be calm. No objection was voiced, although not all were in complete agreement with me. They were all, however, eager to have a report from me on what would take place in class; what the children's questions and comments would be. The parents in turn promised to share with me the children's reactions at home.

The meeting was an occasion for the teacher not only to inform the parents, but to share her own feelings about Rachel's death and its effects on the children. It was an occasion too for the parents to express their concern, to exchange ideas among themselves and, though reluctantly, to face up to their children's encounter with death. The teacher did not resolve the problem but gained some insight and inner strength from the honest discussion with the parents. The parents did not receive definite answers to troubling questions, and they found their comfortable evasions disturbed; yet, they found courage to ask further questions, and opened their minds to a new interest and care in what their children learn from the event of death.

2

"WHAT HAPPENED TO RACHEL?"

I have always liked to include the children in the performance of various teaching chores, among them taking attendance. I have found that children often take notice of the special paper that holds everybody's name and records everybody's presence; they enjoy hearing their names called, and some like telling the teacher "who's missing." Since children usually mention the absentees by name, I expected that Rachel's name would come up, or that someone would ask why she wasn't in class that day. However, no one mentioned Rachel's absence. When I asked, "Who didn't come to school today?" other absent children's names were called out, but not Rachel's. Was it forgotten? Was it omitted on purpose? The same strange silence about Rachel on the second and third day. Why? I felt that the children sensed that something dire, or at least something very uncomfortable had happened and were avoiding confronting the news about Rachel. I then decided to take the initiative of directly eliciting some expression on the subject from the children. I believed it would be healthy for them to speak their minds. It was also important for me to retain rapport with the children and to come forth with what was on my mind.

When, the next day, I sat down with the attendance sheet in front of me, several children came up to join in the familiar task. One child asked casually, "Who's missing today?"

"Maybe you can tell me," I said. In reply someone named an absent child, but no one mentioned Rachel. Taking a deep breath, then, I stated deliberately, "You did not mention another child who is not here," and not getting a prompt reply, I gave a clue, "a girl."

Now in response, a number of children looked up, stopping whatever they were doing, and one of them said quietly, looking at me,

"Rachel is missing."

"Yes," I concurred, trying to control my own emotion. "Rachel isn't here—because something very sad and very unusual happened to her." And rather than saying anything more, I waited for another question.

With a perturbed expression, and more quietly, the same child asked, "What happened to Rachel?"

The painfully brief but clear answer was: "Rachel died—last Monday."

Somehow, every child, although they were scattered in a large room in half-a-dozen different activity areas, did hear it, or at least sensed the significance of what was said by the teacher, for everyone expressed or showed some reaction. For the most part, they continued with what they were doing—painting, drawing, block-building, housekeeping play. For a while, a rather subdued atmosphere prevailed in the room. Some children seemed pensive, some tense. I waited for further response, and soon they began asking questions—thoughtful questions—reflecting deep feeling as well as healthy realism.

The first and obvious question had to do with causes. "Why did Rachel die?" This seemed at first to be an easy question that could be answered factually. Yet the children were not satisfied with the answer ("an unusual sickness that made her stop breathing"). They asked the question again and again, and then made thoughtful comments from their own experience.

"My turtle died because we didn't feed her."

"We had a little dog and he ate some poison and he died." Yes, such things happen, I agreed. The children were thinking still further about Rachel and the causes of death as they knew them in their own lives and on TV, perhaps.

"Maybe somebody shot her," said one child, and another answered, "But nobody would shoot a little child."

Such free expression was tremendously interesting to me. I wanted to hear how the children searched for causes of death that were understandable to them. They now turned to a lighter and, to them, familiar subject, the dangerous doings on the part of children that they imagined might cause death—swallowing wrong objects.

"I swallowed a nickel and I didn't die."

Then came a cheerful contribution. "And my sister swallowed a button! And you know what?" And to the amusement of the children around her, the little girl described the reappearance of the swallowed button in the toilet. Emboldened by such uninhibited talk, some children now mentioned various fantastic objects that they themselves or a member of their family had swallowed with no damage whatsoever. Yes, there was reassurance in those stories about swallowing. And now the subject changed to babies, since most children had younger siblings at home.

"My baby sister was sick and she is all well now."

"My baby brother has five teeth." These and many other observations were made about babies. I knew that they were not all true, but that didn't matter as long as the children were saying what was meaningful to them. Like the swallowing of objects, the stories about babies also seemed to offer some reassurance or comfort to the teller and the listeners.

For a while, the children continued quietly with their activities, but to me the room seemed filled with their thinking about Rachel and as I attended to various chores, I listened for more questions. Presently the most difficult question of all came.

A little girl asked seriously, earnestly, looking me in the eyes, "Will Rachel come back?"

Now I sympathized with the parents and wished I could answer in the affirmative so that everybody would be happy. But this was no time for wishful thinking on my part. The little girl wanted to *know* if Rachel would come back. She wanted to be told the truth, whether she could understand it or not. And though it was difficult to impart knowledge that has such profound implications, I had to do it.

My answer, and it had to be succinct, was, "No, she can't come back." I stopped myself from elaborating, from trying to make the answer somehow easier to comprehend and accept. I wondered how it affected the little girl or the several other children who were definitely listening. The answer soon came. From the other end of the room a boy called out,

"But my brother died and *he* came back to life again. Yes, he did!" This child didn't want any of the teacher's knowledge! And he defended himself against it by the statement that one does come back to life again. That was the knowledge that he could now be comfortable with, not what the teacher said.

All the children heard him and apparently recognized his feeling; they did not contradict him or ask questions. I, too, kept quiet.

Knowledge of death to one's self can be intolerable, even inadmissible, and I was learning that children can give unique expression to such a feeling. A little girl who had only listened and had not offered comments up to then said clearly, perhaps even emphatically,

"My mother doesn't want me to die." A differently stated sense of resisting death—with support of the mother. The other children felt a special accord with this statement. Many turned their heads in her direction as if the little girl had spoken for them, and spoken so completely that they didn't need to add anything. Only the teacher felt compelled to offer reassurance.

"Of course your mother doesn't want you to die."

The children's thinking now turned to another phase of death. A little boy who had listened keenly to the other children's questions now asked his, and to me this was another difficult one.

"Did Rachel's mother cry when Rachel died?"

This question, too, seemed of special interest to a number of children in class, as they listened ever so attentively to my "yes," and a brief account of grief and tears on the part of Rachel's mother as well as other members of her family. I qualified that grown-ups do cry when something sad and hurting happens, then they get over it. Although mentioning Rachel's mother was painful to me, it did not seem so to the children. They appeared only to be interested.

The mood changed as the children turned matter-of-factly to the pursuits at hand. The same boy who spoke of the mother crying, now spoke with the voice of experience; he spoke of realistic adjustment to the event of death.

"When my grandfather died," he said, "my nanny got herself another man."

Other children took in this statement in the same spirit. Someone responded, "Well . . . my grandmother is already in the hospital."

Although another child looked startled for a moment, there was no question as to the implication of what was said. As far as I was concerned, there was no need of further clarification. The children had reacted fully to my sharing of the tragic news that their classmate Rachel had died. They showed feeling about their own protection from death, they showed empathy with grief and some realism about adjustment for the living.

I felt that the atmosphere in the room was conducive to free communication on the part of the children, and that I didn't need to elicit further questions or expressions of concern. My own concern was with further communication with the parents.

Later the same morning, when talking about Rachel had stopped and the children seemed involved in finishing various works and commencing the easily interruptible cleanup, the door opened and in walked one of the mothers.* It was Carol's mother. To my surprise and to the mother's shock, the children (en masse it seemed) rushed up to Carol's mother, bursting with exclamations and a spontaneous choral chant.

"Rachel died," repeating the phrase over and over. The mother was practically in tears to see such an unrestrained, noisy, and, to her, crude utterance. I had to calm the children down emphatically and tell them that this way of telling about Rachel would not do because it bothered Carol's mother. Yet it appeared to me, and I shared my thinking with Carol's mother and other parents, that the children's exuberant expression showed that they *cared.* The noise and the expressive chant were the children's natural way of letting off accumulated tension from the news, their way of *sharing* a significant experience with the first person they encountered. Surely we can't expect little children to behave with restraint and to utter proper words to suit the occasion.

Sharing the news of Rachel's death with their parents proved to be very important to the children.

"Does my mother know Rachel died?" was the first concern of one child after Carol's mother left. "Yes." Then the other children promptly asked, "Did you tell *my* mother, too?"

I told them about talking with all their mothers and fathers.

That day many of the children announced the news excitedly to their parents as soon as they got home. Others told it after a few days had elapsed. Perhaps those children needed time to absorb the knowledge, to think about it first. One little boy, a generally quiet

*At this school, parents were free to visit without making appointments.

child, said nothing about the event until three weeks had passed, and then, during dinner with company, he was overwhelmed by an urge to talk about it. He leaned toward his mother and whispered the news to her; the mother promptly whispered back, and only after doing it said, "Excuse us," to the rest of the people at the table. Such incidents of children holding something important in their minds for a long time are not uncommon. It wasn't that the child didn't care or forgot the incident; rather, it took time to absorb the important knowledge and finally have the urge to share it.

In school, the children kept bringing the subject up over a period of many weeks. Rather than dismiss or forget they seemed to store information in their minds till it was time for unburdening.

"My mother told me about deadness. When you die they put you far away from where people live."

"Yes, there is a special place like that," I confirmed. "It's called a cemetery." Other children claimed to have seen a cemetery. And that was all that could be said on the subject.

Yet, another subject, related to the concern of what follows physical death, did hold the children's serious attention and elicited compassion. Appreciative as I was of the children's feelings, I was still surprised by the depth of the child's question. Looking at the class attendance list in the teacher's hands shortly after the news of Rachel's death, a child asked, "Should Rachel's name be scratched off the list?" Not answering her directly, I addressed myself to the others nearby.

"What do you think, children—should we scratch Rachel's name off the list? Or leave it?" And, as at other times, one child expressed a feeling that others also had.

"Don't scratch the name off. So we can keep it for remembrance." And some children related this act of "remembrance" at home. Thus, Rachel's name was left on the class list where it had been, "unscratched." And in deference to Rachel the school administration followed the children's lead and did not fill Rachel's place in the class for the remaining months of the term as would have been done if she had simply been withdrawn from school. Clearly what they had learned from acknowledging Rachel's death, expressing feelings of sadness, worry, and denial of death, as well as mentioning the practical consequences, was enormous. The children's initial reticence and silence did *not* signify to the teacher that the matter was not important, as it gave way to questions and assertions about death. The teacher then learned how responsive children can be when she relates a significant happening to them, and how individual they are in their responses. She found out how acute the children were in their psychological reaction: denial of death, recognition of a mother's special grief; making blithe, joking comments for diversion from worry, and shouting uninhibitedly to relieve tension.

The informal classroom discussion afforded the children an experience of mutual expression of feeling about death, of having the teacher's honest answers, and of her telling them only what they wanted to know about death. The parents learned that there is mutual benefit in talking with young children in a simple, sympathetic manner about death when it occurs; that children can bear such knowledge.

3

"DOES THE WORLD STOP?"

Nursery-school teachers have an unusual opportunity to hear and record children's spontaneous conversations that may reveal thinking and groping for understanding, including an understanding of death. We find this in Evelyn Beyer's article, "Language Learning—Fresh, Vivid, and Their Own." The article quotes four- and five-year-old children who engage spontaneously in a dialogue about life and death.

> *Robert:* You know what, Brian? I don't want to go to war and get killed.
> *Brian:* The docs and nurses wouldn't let you get killed.
> *Robert:* When you're dead, you can't breathe.
> *Brian:* How about when someone stepped on you when you were dead? (giggling)
> *Robert:* You wouldn't know it.
> *Brian:* I would; I'd have feelings.
> *Robert:* No you wouldn't. You can't feel anything. (to the teacher) What happens when you are dead?
> *Teacher:* You just stop breathing and living.

Brian: Does the world stop?
Teacher: No, the world goes on.
Robert: But you get life again in heaven!
Teacher: How do you know?
Robert: It says in the Bible! Ever after! I have a Bible, and I know![1]

Such striving to know the concrete aspects of death ("breathing" and "feeling"), such desire for self-protection ("don't want to go to war"), and the wish for life to go on "forever after."

Here are further reports by Miss Beyer.

Jeff was pushing a big boat across the floor toward Ann's building.
Jeff: Here comes the big old battleship!
Ann: Oh, Jeff, don't say the word of "battle." It reminds me of killing people, and I can't stand the word of it!
Jeff: Oh all right, it was an old battleship of the civilized war, and now it's just for people, plain people, and there is no killing allowed.
Ann: Good, I'm glad!

And on the same theme, comments after Gingerbread, a guinea pig, died.

Bobby: Gingerbread went to the church, his laboratory. They gave him a pill, you know, aspirin. But it didn't make him better. And so he died because he couldn't eat any food. He couldn't ever come back.
Danny: I think he's dead at the church.
Bobby: I hope he comes back.

1. Evelyn Beyer, "Language Learning—Fresh, Vivid, and Their Own," *Childhood Education,* October 1971, p. 21.

Danny: Bobby, you know he can't.
Bobby: I said, I hope.
Danny: Well, he can't!²

Speaking freely, the children are trying to figure out what does happen in death—no breathing, no eating. And no coming back? Well, at least we can "hope." Children understand hope!

What was educationally meaningful in Miss Beyer's article was that the children's expressions were "their own." They were speaking in their own language, and originally at that, while groping for meaning in their own experiences: "[he] went to the church," "they gave him a pill." They asked their own profound question: "Does the world stop?" And what they said and questioned was enough at the time. Later, with more experience and mental growth, children will want to know more; but at this stage, unless specific questions are asked, adult information would be redundant.

Parents and teachers need not wait for spontaneous conversation about death to take place. An occasion for children to talk about death can be provided by a good children's book, a book that is a work of art in its literary qualities and appeal, yet one in which the author presents death honestly and understandably to children. Such a book is invariably interesting to a wide age range, as well as to the adult.

The Tenth Good Thing about Barney by Judith Viorst is artistically original in narrative style, in theme, and mood.³ In the story a boy is sad because his cat Barney

2. Ibid., p. 22.
3. Judith Viorst, *The Tenth Good Thing about Barney* (New York: Atheneum, 1971).

has died. By attention to the burial, the enumeration of realistic "good things about Barney"—while the usual activities and relationships go on—the boy's sadness slowly works itself out. In the story, through the parents' low-key sympathy with the boy's sadness and his recognition of "the tenth good thing," the sadness finally gives way to an appreciation of living, and a new concept about nature. "Barney is in the ground and he's helping grow flowers."

A group of five-, six-, and seven-year-olds reflect their understanding of the theme as they listen to the story, *The Tenth Good Thing about Barney,* a small picture book, read by a visitor. Children, whatever age, usually respond to a picture book by being at least as much interested in the pictures as in the story. In this case, however, though the small, charming, black-and-white illustrations were shown, the children scarcely bothered to look. They were listening, imagining, thinking, and expressing thoughts.

The visitor read: "'At night I still didn't want to watch any television.'" Then she stopped and asked, "Why didn't the boy want to watch television?"

"He was *sad* that Barley died," a child answered readily, emphasizing "sad" and stumbling on the name. A child next to her corrected, "Not Barley, Barney was the cat that died." And the first child restated her comment, making the correction, again being especially clear in saying the word "sad." In using this simple word throughout the story the author conveyed not only the feeling but what one does and what one refrains from doing when saddened by death; the little boy was not watching television, not eating much. This did not seem morbid to the children, but understandable and interesting. Also interesting to them was an intense argument in the story: the boy's friend Annie contended that "Barney was in heaven with lots of cats and angels," while the boy was convinced that Barney was definitely in the ground. Apparently visualizing heaven as a remote place, one of the children gave her opinion.

"It takes a long time to get to heaven."

Another child, having the notion that heaven is above, responded to that, "But how do you get to heaven from the ground?" And herself gave the answer, "You must climb and jump up," demonstrating with movement a heavenward ascent. Then an "agnostic" spoke just as freely.

"Some people don't believe in heaven." But no one argued with her. And the child who first spoke about heaven turned realist.

"In the ground there are worms and bugs and things—and they eat up what's dead."

"I don't like to see dead. All that . . . (a grimace) and it makes me *sad*." Perhaps she was using the word from the book.

Listening to the story provided an occasion for the children to talk about the sadness caused by death, and to reflect about "heaven," and earth with "bugs and things."

Children identify with the story, *The Tenth Good Thing about Barney*—with the modern child in the story, with his experience of losing a pet, his expression of feelings about death. The child reader, affected by the story, will absorb some comprehensible truth about death, perhaps have thoughts of his own, and will want to ask questions.

To share a children's book with one child or a few is

a unique challenge and delight to an adult or to an older child. You yourself may find a children's book surprisingly interesting, once you've become acquainted with it. Reading with a child, whether he or she is still unable to read or has already acquired the skill, means finding stimulation, beauty, and a new understanding by means of a book. A book with the theme of death can lead to talking about a subject that is otherwise difficult for parent or child.

As numerous studies and reports from psychologists (notably Elisabeth Kübler-Ross[4]), as well as articles by educators, have appeared, showing the need for intelligent recognition of death and openness in learning about it, parents' interest in the subject as well as children's awareness have grown. Now, a great number of children's books published in the last decade deal with the subject of death.

Some books deal with encounters with dead animals. Finding a dead bird is a quite common and touching experience that involves convincing evidence of death. It often elicits melancholy and poetic reflection in children. And in children's literature there are books dealing with children's responses to the death of a bird.

Margaret Wise Brown, who depicted so successfully children's true feelings in her books, tells in *The Dead Bird* about children finding a dead bird, attending to the burial, and performing an impressive, sad funeral.[5] This simple, stark story was criticized as not appropriate for children when it was published several decades ago, but is now entirely acceptable to librarians and parents,

4. Elisabeth Kübler-Ross, *On Death and Dying* (New York: Macmillan Co., 1976).

5. Margaret Wise Brown, *The Dead Bird* (Reading, Mass.: Addison-Wesley, 1958).

for there is no longer a taboo against death (or any theme about life's troubles) being presented in children's books. A recent book, *When Violet Died,* also deals with a children's funeral ceremony and burial of a dead bird.[6] Reading about burial and funerals, children get a notion of the finality of death, and of the spirit and form that must accompany it. Even vicarious participation in a ritual with its drama and ceremony, and attention to the act and mystery of burial appeals to children and helps them perceive the essentially human attributes of death.

Annie and the Old One is an unusual book of literary distinction.[7] It presents a child's frightening knowledge of her beloved grandmother's imminent death. Here, depicting the culture and traditions by which the Navajos live, the author and artist portray the strengths, the spirit and companionship of an old Indian grandmother who talks of her approaching death. "My children, when the new rug is taken from the loom, I will go to Mother Earth." Annie, rejecting passionately her grandmother's demise, is determined to prevent it. She resorts to extraordinary means to keep her mother occupied away from the loom. She even unravels half of the weaving that had been done, so the rug will not get finished and taken from the loom. But the grandmother at last convinces Annie of the inevitability of change and time in nature's cycle. Annie then accepts the continued rug weaving, and helps with its necessary completion. Grandmother's death doesn't actually occur, but the inevitability of it is inescapable, and the reader feels empathy for Annie in her vehement rejection of the death

6. Mildred Kantrowitz, *When Violet Died* (New York: Parents Press, 1973).
7. Miska Miles, *Annie and the Old One* (Boston: Little, Brown, 1971).

of her grandmother, and her clever though useless tricks to avoid it. With Annie, the reader also arrives at the eventual (and wise) perception of the whole cycle of life and death.

A more recent artistic book on the theme of love and companionship between a child and a grandparent and happy remembrance after death is *My Grandson Lew*.[8]

Some children's books about death and grief are of pointedly psychological nature. *My Grandpa Died Today* acquaints the child reader directly with human death, with a child's feeling of loss, with recovery from grief, and the return to lively activity.[9]

Specifically helpful to parents in answering children's concrete questions, or to older children to read by themselves are the clearly informational books. In *Life and Death* the authors offer factual biological information on birth, on the emergence of living forms, the life spans of different creatures, aging, the process and proof of death, as well as relative causes of death through the ages.[10] There is information on regulations for burial and on various cultural and religious beliefs pertaining to the dead. Finally, the authors present the specific ecological view of the necessity for death.

Sharing books, parents and children can learn together the truth (or aspects of truth) about death which can serve as preparation for understanding and coping with death when it occurs. It is also possible that sharing books can lead to a realization that with death "the world doesn't stop."

8. Charlotte Zolotow, *My Grandson Lew* (New York: Harper & Row, 1974).

9. Joan Fassler, *My Grandpa Died Today* (New York: Behavioral Publications, 1971).

10. Herbert S. Zim and Sonia Bleeker, *Life and Death* (New York: William R. Morrow, 1970).

4

"WHO DEADED HIM?"

Children's Experiences with the
Death of Animals

While learning about death from a book may be informative to both children and adults, may lead to increased awareness, and serve as preparation for direct experience, it is direct experience with death that especially concerns us. The questions we are endeavoring to answer are: Should children know about death directly? And what is the effect of such knowledge?

Although this book begins with the death of Rachel, since that incident prompted the writing of it, and there will be discussion of children's experiences with human death in a subsequent chapter, it is important for now to consider children's encounters with the death of animals. Such encounters may serve both children and parents as a preparatory step in coping with the death and loss of humans.

Children of all ages love animals. All of us know many instances of a child's tender relationship with a pet, while adult and children's literature abounds with stories of such relationships between children and their animal friends of all kinds and sizes. The incomparable A. A. Milne shows us a small child's devotion to a mere beetle whom he calls Alexander and shelters in a match box. The child is most distressed when he loses him and is sure that he and the beetle recognize each other![1]

For an older child, living with and caring for, and yes, worrying about a pet, means a rich involvement that may be remembered for life.

Alicia was about seven when she had the thrill of acquiring a mongrel puppy whom she named Fluffy. It instantly elicited the tenderest of feelings and became a source of companionship, amusement, new concerns, and startling discoveries. "No, I don't want Fluffy to get spayed—I want her to have babies!" Later, Alicia was beside herself with worry that her small Fluffy might have mated with a large neighborhood dog and might die giving birth to big puppies. "How can you be sure? Can the doctor help now?"

Then one snow-stormy afternoon, when Fluffy was four years old, she was hit by a car as she emerged from a snowbank, in view of the horrified Alicia and her mother. They spared no effort in getting Fluffy to the hospital where the diagnosis was internal injuries and broken bones. The doctor had given up on Fluffy, and asked, "Are you really attached to that dog? Because . . ." Alicia was most indignant at the question. *She* remained hopeful and wanted medical treatment for her pet. When Fluffy did not improve in the hospital and refused food, Alicia wanted to take care of her at home.

1. A. A. Milne, "Forgiven" in *Now We Are Six* (New York: E. P. Dutton, 1954).

Miraculously, it seemed, the dog indeed responded to her hand feeding and personal nursing! In a few weeks Fluffy was perfectly well and running about, except for a slight limp from the fractured hip.

Such involvement in caring for an animal, in responding to trouble and nursing it *in spite* of medical failure, is bound to teach responsibility and compassion (whether the animal survives or dies) as few other experiences can; it is bound to have an effect on a child's human growth, on values in later life.

When a dog is actually killed in a car accident, which is not an uncommon occurrence, and it happens to be a child's pet, the child may suffer deeply. A child's grief over the death of a dog killed by a truck is portrayed starkly in a recent children's book *The Accident.*[2] Christopher, the boy, is furiously angry at the driver though it is not the driver's fault. The boy is torn by remorse for having taken the dog out that evening; he pretends that the dog didn't die after all. He yells angry accusing words at his father for burying the dog. "Why did you go and bury him without me?" His parents are patient and entirely sympathetic with the boy's grief. Then his father takes him to a place to pick out a stone for the dog's grave. When Christopher finally talks with his father about the dog and sobs freely, and then places the stone as a marker on the grave, the reader feels that Christopher's grief is over. Such a somber story doesn't make for "fun" reading, but it does illuminate a child's grief over the death of a pet, and describes realistically the family's part in it. Such a story would be especially helpful for children and parents who have had similar experiences.

2. Carol Carrick, *The Accident* (New York: Seabury Press, 1976).

In an article, "They Learn from Living Things," the anthropologist Margaret Mead discusses the profoundly educational value of giving children an opportunity to care for and observe animals, to have contact with the whole cycle of life, including death. Modern children, she contends, deal mostly with toys and lifeless mechanical things which they manipulate and command. They therefore need to balance (or counteract) this with learning humility from living plants and animals. Living creatures have their own rhythms and demands which a child learns to satisfy and adapt to, and this teaches humility. Dr. Mead further explains that from having living creatures around the modern child learns the meaning of death. Children may see a good deal of killing on TV, but not have actual experience with death. As children seldom have an opportunity to see dying or dead human beings, "they must become deeply familiar with the life cycles—from birth to natural or accidental death—of other living things, if they are to gain that deep respect for life, awe in the face of death on which civilization rests."[3]

Parents generally look with favor on their children having a pet, on their getting to know and care about a healthy living creature. But if the creature should die, the attitude changes from appreciating the child's relationship with the animal to denial and even deviousness. Parents, relatives, teachers, and adult friends of the family usually do not want children to know about the demise of the animal they've known and cared about. Most adults wish to conceal not only the animal remains from children but the very knowledge of death in gen-

3. Margaret Mead, "They Learn from Living Things," *Parents' Magazine*, February 1961, p. 84.

eral. Perhaps the dead animal brings to mind our own mortality which we try to deny, or we may assume the dead animal will cause unnecessary distress to the otherwise happy children. It is commonplace for adults to avoid a child's encounter with the death of animals.

When Ann was about eight years old, her parents presented her with a beautiful caged parakeet. Though they were not animal lovers themselves, the parents recognized the value of the daily attention given to and pleasure received from a pet. They felt, too, that a pet would provide companionship for an only child, and that the beauty of the colorful bird would be especially attractive to artistic Ann. They were right. Ann loved the lively bird, promptly named it Lollypop, and helped in the care of it with diligence and delight.

When Ann and her parents went on a vacation, they left Lollypop with a trusted aunt. And, although the aunt kept Lollypop in the kitchen where the door could be shut securely while the cat was around, tragedy occurred. The cat found a way to slip into the kitchen and left telltale feathers around an open, empty cage. Ann's parents, upon learning the news, knew exactly what to do. Never would they tell Ann that her pet was eaten alive. How monstrous. How utterly abhorrent. They couldn't possibly be so cruel as to tell Ann the truth of what happened. And what for? Why have her suffer grief if it could be avoided? It seemed quite simple for them to tell her that Lollypop had flown out of an accidentally opened window and might well have been caught and adopted as a pet by some kindly soul.

Ann believed her parents' story about the bird's disappearance, and according to them she was not upset. Quite soon afterward, her parents provided Ann with a replacement. Recalling the incident as an adult, Ann says, "I never thought that he was dead. I was sad and worried, but very hopeful that someone was taking care of him, someplace. Then my parents bought me another parakeet. I don't think that was my idea; you can't replace a lost bird with another, really. But after a while I got to like Lollypop Junior, too."

Ann's sensitive reflection, "You can't replace a lost bird with another, really," constitutes an important observation. It shows how one's caring for a creature (or a person) and one's loyalty to it don't normally allow for an immediate replacement. Such rushing to replace denies feelings of loss and of needed time for a new allegiance.

There are two important assumptions here which we shall question. One is the parents' assumption that what is abhorrent to them is abhorrent and damaging to the child; that their duty, therefore, is to protect the child from it. In reality, cats hunting birds is an old story and when a child learns about this aspect of nature, he may be very distressed and puzzled. Losing a pet by such a law of nature could be most shocking (as Ann's parents had surmised). But must we *always* protect children from being shocked? Besides, Ann was not a fragile but a quite realistic child. At age five she dictated the following:

> November and Thanksgiving
>> Have come along.
> I feel sorry for the turkeys
>> Who used to sing such an ugly song.
> But November and Thanksgiving
>> Have come along.

We all know that children have remarkable stamina in confronting even greater tragedy, provided they can share the experience with people they love, if they are free to express feelings, and, if possible, do something on their own initiative. Such experience of shock and sorrow, of sharing and consequent learning would be likely to have a positive and maturing effect on a child.

The other questionable assumption is that a child will never know that you are not telling the truth. Perhaps one can be clever and convincing enough to succeed (as did Ann's parents). Also, with ordinary, inconsequential matters, truth can be withheld for the adults' convenience. However, when it comes to something important—and the death of a pet is—an evasion is unlikely to register as truth to the child's psyche, and thus is apt to hinder a trusting relationship. On the other hand, telling the truth—in spite of the fact that it is difficult and painful to do so—and telling it not abruptly or matter-of-factly but honestly and sensitively can signify confidence, trust, and a new turn in the relationship of parent and child. The parents and child who have gone through the trauma of the death of a pet together may gain strength and wisdom to endure a more significant trauma at another time.

We turn now from the intensity and profound effect of the one-to-one, private relationship between a child and her pet animal to a sharing experience with animals in a group of four- to five-year-olds in a private school.

A teacher who allows the children experiences with living creatures must be prepared for consequences that may not always be pleasant but are entirely possible.

Mrs. Clark could not resist some baby chicks which

were available in the local pet shop. She bought six of them and installed them in a proper wire cage. After attention to food and shelter, several children had an enjoyable discussion about naming them, and finally decided upon: Chicky, Nicky, Ricky, Picky, Squeaky, and Petunia. After only two days there was an unexpected loss. One chick died, possibly from cold. After an inspection it was established that there was a draft in the classroom; the maintenance man was consulted and an electric bulb was attached to the cage to provide warmth, which the children understood was necessary for baby chicks' health. "It's a good thing that electricity works," one child observed. And with the interest in providing vital warmth for the five lively, growing chicks, the death of the sixth did not arouse more than passing concern. Then another loss occurred which provided a different science lesson. Picky became droopy and would not eat. The children had watched the chicks so closely that they quickly noticed that "something is wrong with this one." This time another member of the school staff, who had had experience on a chicken farm, was consulted, and her advice of isolating the sick chick so that others would not succumb was promptly followed. The next day there was intense interest in preserving the health of the four chicks and also in observing the dying chick, which could no longer run or rise or take the eagerly proffered drinks of water.

Before the chick stopped breathing, the children made plans for burying him. Richard took a box and put it next to the chicken to see if he would fit in it. The children on the whole were quite matter-of-fact about the death and burial of Picky. They did, however, seem extra watchful and more protective towards the others than they had been before. But one emotional little girl, five-year-old Helen, was upset by the chick's death, cried a little in class, and watched the other chicks anxiously, saying frequently, "I hope *they* don't die." During that week she dreamt of another of the chicks dying and conveyed her worry to her family. The teacher was sympathetic towards Helen and assured her that the other chicks were healthy and would receive good care; she kept herself from becoming sentimental and from contributing to Helen's distress. Helen soon became particularly devoted to the four chicks who grew to be fast-running young chickens and were transferred to a large enclosure outdoors. There the chickens provided endless entertainment by trying to take worms away from one another. Before the end of the year, the surviving chickens were returned to the pet shop owner as originally agreed.

Were the deaths a shocking exposure to the children? And should the teacher have concealed them or at least prevented the children from observing dying animals? This teacher herself was not so shocked by the incident of infant mortality among baby chicks, and she felt confident that reasonably good care was provided for the animals. It seemed to her that the natural death of an animal does provide children with important facts of life and that handling such a situation as it occurs, without denying the feeling of loss or regret, or the knowledge of pertinent facts, will provide a wholesome rather than a morbid or worrisome experience for children.[4]

We see in the record the children's natural response to and their practical-scientific interest in maintaining chicks, as well as their readiness to face the inevitable occurrence of death. We see the range in individual children's reactions from Richard's matter-of-fact measuring of the coffin to genuine distress on the part

---

4. Dorothy H. Cohen and Marguerita Rudolph, *Kindergarten and Early Schooling* (Englewood Cliffs, N.J.: Prentice-Hall, 1977), pp. 192–93.

of Helen, a child who frequently found cause for tearful outbursts. Knowing this, the teacher controlled her empathy toward her, but saw to it that Helen was a participant not only in the burial but in the care of the living chicks as well. The burial made the death of the animal final and over with.

In another situation, a different reaction to a dead animal occurred in a class of younger children.

> The teacher discovers one morning that one of the two frogs she has recently acquired is dead; but before discarding it she leaves it in a bowl next to the enclosed live one. She knows the children would miss the frog and would ask to see it, in whatever state.
>
> Roger, three and a half, comes up to the frog and asks: "Why is this frog here?"
>
> "This frog is dead," the teacher answers.
>
> *Roger:* Who deaded him?
>
> *Teacher:* Nobody did anything to him. He died by himself.
>
> *Roger:* Why did he die?
>
> *Teacher:* He jumped out of the mud pan and we couldn't find him; so he had no mud or water, and he dried up and died. (The teacher tries to be simple, accurate and brief.)
>
> *Roger:* Is this frog dead?
>
> *Teacher:* Yes.
>
> *Roger:* Put him in water.
>
> *Teacher:* It won't do him any good.
>
> *Roger:* (still only looking intently and not touching the frog) Will he bite?
>
> *Teacher:* No.
>
> *Roger:* (apparently unable to understand the fact of death) Why is the frog dead?
>
> *Teacher:* He dried up and died.

Roger: Can I put him on the table? (He handles the frog rather cautiously, places him on his back on the table, and asks again) Isn't the frog dead?
Teacher: Yes.
Roger: (touching and inspecting the frog's belly) Can he turn over?
Teacher: The frog is dead, so he can't do anything.
Roger: Give him some food.
Teacher: No, the frog can't eat—he's dead.
Roger: Why is he dead?
Teacher: He had no water or mud, so he dried up.
Roger: I'll turn him over.

As he does so, Roger seems to realize that the frog is incapable of resistance or reaction (certainly different from the jumpy, live one he had finally made himself touch). But he pokes the dead frog and seems to be watching for reaction and asks still again: "Is the frog dead?" The teacher answers him, realizing that a child needs innumerable repetitions of the same question as well as time to understand a complicated matter. Not only the physical fact, but the acceptance of death, is complicated for a child.

After almost half an hour of studying the dead frog, Roger picks it up and brings it to the children at another table, who are using clay, and have not shown an interest in the dead frog thus far. Roger says to them:

"See, this frog is dead." Then he brings the frog to Albert who is block-building, and says, "See, Albert, this frog is dead because he didn't have any water." Albert merely responds with a look of recognition, and Roger takes the frog back to the table, where more and shared inspection of it takes place. Several other children ask, "Who deaded him?" and they advise placing it in water, supposedly to resuscitate it. Roger continues watching, and does not want to relinquish the dead frog to other children or to the teacher. When the housekeeper enters the classroom with milk and cookies, Roger grasps the dead frog and rushes over to her excitedly:

"Miss Farrell! Look! This frog is dead; he didn't have any mud and he didn't have any water, so he dried up and he *died*." He says it with intensity and importance, while the teacher is listening to her own words accurately and aptly repeated by Roger. But in spite of the accurate words, the teacher does not think that Roger really understands the complicated phenomenon of the cessation of life, or that he won't ask about it again when another occasion presents itself.

Roger's attentions to the dead frog may appear at first as sheer persistence, but on second thought they show considerable intellectual effort, and his gradual way of communicating information.[5]

Again we see the great individual differences in children. There seemed to be a total lack of interest or observation on the part of all the other children. Yet, on the part of Roger, there was distinct intellectual curiosity, persistent inquiry, cautious handling of the dead frog, and finally an attempt at explaining death. Throughout the incident, Roger was sharing his knowledge with others in a reasonable manner. The important facts were that the teacher did not assume that *all* the children must learn some "lesson" from the dead frog, and that she was content to answer Roger's questions briefly and to the point only. She also observed his attention to specific anatomical-physiological details, typical of the way young children learn. However, she

5. Marguerita Rudolph, *Living and Learning in Nursery School* (New York: Harper Bros., 1954), pp. 112–14.

had deliberately left the dead frog in a place where it would be noticed by anyone who was interested. Other teachers feel differently, as is shown in the following episode.

A young nursery school teacher came into the director's office with a confused, unnatural expression on her face.

"There is a—hum—dead gerbil in our room," she said to the director. "Shall I ask the custodian to take him away? Or do you want to do something about it?"

This teacher had warm feelings for each child in her class and intelligent interest in every aspect of learning that went on in the group. However, she could not bring herself to handle animals, dead or alive; she only tolerated their presence for the children's sake.

"Frankly," the teacher added anxiously, "the sooner it's out of the room . . . the children don't seem to be a bit interested anyway. Nobody came up to the cage or said anything."

She spoke quite rationally. Still, the director was not convinced of the children's indifference. She went into the room and took the cage from its corner and placed it near the children.

"I want to see your gerbil," she said to whomever was within hearing distance.

Immediately, a couple of children also wanted "to see." When they asked what was the matter with the gerbil, the answer was: "What do you think?" A number of thoughtful answers were given by the group who by now had gathered around the gerbil. "He is sleeping." "He is resting." "He is sick." "He can't move." "Maybe he is dead."

Leslie nodded, confirming the last answer. "He is dead all right."

"Let's see him," some children said.

When the dead gerbil was placed on the table, a little boy moved him gently with a finger and said seriously, "See—he can move. He's not dead."

Many children wanted to touch the dead gerbil and they offered proof of death. Some assumed the gerbil would be cured with food and water. Others wanted burial like the "Dead Bird" in the story by Margaret Wise Brown. Some were skeptical about finality.

"Let's see what happens by the time we have snack. Let's wait till then," insisted Leslie.

It was evident by now, especially with Leslie's refrain, "He's dead all right," that attention to the dead animal had lasted long enough.

"You are right," the adult in charge said to the children with finality. "The gerbil is dead. And we can bury him in a good spot in our yard when we go out." And they did![6]

The children wrapped the dead gerbil protectively in some cloth, dug the grave in a selected spot under a tree, and while some children did the work others formed a circle of serious quiet watchers. The teacher, in spite of her reluctance to be in any way involved with the dead animal herself, appreciated the value of the experience to the children.

Many teachers, and parents, would have a similar attitude toward a small dead animal: disposing of it expediently, and forgetting about it; being busy with other, pleasanter things. Doing this may of course be convenient for adults, but it denies children an opportunity to learn firsthand what "dead" means.

6. Marguerita Rudolph, *From Hand to Head* (New York: Schocken Books, 1977), pp. 27–28.

Entirely different from natural and accidental death is the deliberate killing of animals which even small children may inadvertently witness. Adults usually and sensibly avoid exposing children to such a sight. Yet, the possibility of such an encounter exists, as we can see in the following experience.

The episode took place on a working farm connected with a boarding school. Although the teacher of the youngest, the five- to seven-year-old group, was always to be notified in advance when a butchering would take place, someone had forgotten the notification. When the small group was on a brief outing between classes, they came upon the strung-up carcass of a calf attended by two men. The seeming enormity of the exposed carcass (as compared to the lively, living calf) and the bloody, messy, *strange* insides of the animal were a shock to the teacher and the children alike. The teacher's immediate reaction was to get the children away and avoid their possible distress as well as the difficult-to-answer questions. But that was impossible. The children did not respond to the teacher's request to leave or to her reminder that a special treat was waiting for them. They were completely fascinated by the butchering scene and would not budge. In order to know what to do next, the teacher turned to a rational appraisal of the situation.

"Children," she called urgently, "this butchering is important *work,* and you mustn't be in the men's way." They understood this. Indeed they didn't want "blood on clothes," or to be "chased away," they said. They thus retreated to a proper distance but still in view of the butchering. As these were all city children, who did not know about butchering as a usual source of food, the teacher wanted to make sure the children understood that this work meant food production—meat for dinner which they all liked. No question on that score. Practically all the questions were anatomical: the names and locations of the lungs, the liver, and other internal organs. The hide, which they called "skin," was carefully observed. What seemed to make the greatest impression on that group of children was the removal of the hide. And as they played a game of "butchering" later, the process of "skinning" was attended to with graphic gestures. The interest in anatomy that had started with the butchering lasted for a considerable time and was useful to the teacher in planning her program and obtaining appropriate reference books.

Susan Isaacs, the British authority on childhood psychology and education, describes children's intellectual curiosity as they observe, in their own environment, living and dead animals.[7] She explains their interest in "cutting a dead animal to see the inside," as biological investigation. She also refers to a child's toughness about the destruction of a suffering animal, and advises adults to be tough in order to be *humane* and realistic about animals. The adults' role is to help children to know and to respect nature; help them recognize the purposefulness and constructiveness of their acts, as in the case of dissection, or in the case of killing harmful insects for protection. Isaacs believes it is important for children to become familiar with the biological facts of death by having animals around informally, with an opportunity to care for them, to study them, to express interest freely without fear of adult taboos.

7. Susan Isaacs, *Intellectual Growth in Young Children* (New York: Schocken Books, 1966).

Biological facts of death can also be perceived when children have experience in caring for plants, which means getting to know living, growing, flowering, bearing, and finally dead plants in a relatively short time. By having contact with plants indoors and out, children become familiar with the conditions for life: nourishment, light, and air; protection from cold and heat. They become familiar with the phenomena of growth and of propagation; familiar with problems such as infestation, disease, accidents, and, not unlikely, encounters with death. The terminology for the life and death of plants is the same as it is for other living things: a frost that "killed the crops"; a neglected house plant that "dies"; removal of dry, "dead" potato plants after they have grown and produced numerous healthy potatoes which can, in turn, be planted to produce another crop, thus starting another cycle. Flowers with their beauty of color, form, and scent "live" but a few days, then wilt and "die." This is discernible to children and suggests the concept of inevitable changes in nature. A tree living for many years and providing shelter and food for thousands of creatures succumbs and comes to the end of its own life. Yet, children can also see a graphic demonstration of how dead plants contribute to life and how nothing in nature is wasted.[8]

Experiences with living things, including dying plants, will lead children to a recognition of the life cycle, and to a gradual understanding of human death. Children, being responsive to and interacting with living things about them, both at home and in school situations, acquire fundamental knowledge of the biological

8. Alvin Tresselt, *The Dead Tree* (New York: Parents Press, 1972).

process. Such knowledge naturally includes encounters with death in nature, whether the death of plants or a loved pet. With adults' recognition of children's interest, and with sensitivity to their feelings and experiences with the death of animals, comes an appreciation of living and a strengthening of humane values. Such experiences lead also to gradual understanding of human death.

5

"THE SADDEST DAY OF MY LIFE"

The Death of Family Members

Many adults, inclined to keep children from encounters with the death of animals, also wish to spare them from knowledge about the death of a particular person, as in the case of Rachel. When there is death in the family, most adults, desiring to protect the children, shield them from the experience of loss, from expression of grief, and from participation in mourning. Yet children, being family members, have the same need as adults to be part of, to be included in the knowledge of what happened, and to be involved in some relevant activity. To be excluded because of age or status diminishes one's sense of membership, one's sense of self. Children who are excluded or isolated when there is death in the family are likely to suffer confusion and be unable to cope with the tragedy which they can *sense* has occurred.

The popular media in recent years have been presenting evidence and advice on the wisdom of open, honest handling of death with children, and the attitude of our society toward death is now changing. However, many people who have been brought up on taboos against discussing death with children find it difficult to change their attitudes.

Besides being protective at a time of tragedy, adults may also be too involved in their own despair to heed the children's needs; they may even become less attentive to the children and to the accustomed secure routines. The child in the bereaved family is then confronted with the need to cope not only with the loss of the family member who died, but with the changed (seemingly estranged) behavior of the living people who are important to him. One mother, crying with grief over the death of her husband, realized her young daughter's distress at the sight of a now different mother, and took pains to assure the child that she, the mother, would not always be tearful and sad; that in time she would return to being an attentive mother, to being herself. How important the communication was for the child and for the mother!

Letting *children* in on the activities and the sorrow surrounding the death of a family member who is close to a child can be of help to the adults themselves as well as to the child. Despite the inevitable disruption that comes with death in the family, there need not be destruction of close family life; and though slow and difficult, recovery from loss naturally takes place when there is open sharing and specific help to a child. We see this in some modern American children's literature in the form of realistic fiction for school-age children.

Virginia Lee conveys this with artistry and imagination in *The Magic Moth*.[1] In a rather unusual family with five children and various animals, ten-year-old Maryanne has been in bed for a year with a fatal heart ailment from which she continues to grow weaker. Everyone in the family, including the youngest, five-year-old Mark-O, does something to take care of Maryanne—bringing food, surprises, and entertainment. In reply to questions, father tells the children the truth: the doctors can no longer do anything to cure Maryanne. The implication is clear to all, including Mark-O. He has been especially friendly with his ailing sister, showing great concern and eagerness to know just what her condition is. Does she *look* like someone who's going to die? Will she come back after she dies? He asks his mother; and he asks questions of other members of the family—sometimes to their annoyance, especially that of his older brother. Though Maryanne is no longer able to tell him stories the way she used to, Mark-O continues his lively communications, bringing her simple presents—a small rock, a bug, a cocoon in a jar—and Maryanne smiles with appreciation. He also plants a sprouted grapefruit seed in a pot for her. As he digs dirt out of the ground for the seed, he feels the coldness and asks his mother if William, the guinea pig, which had been buried in the ground, *minds* being in the cold, and the mother says no, he doesn't feel anything anymore. "Is that what will happen to Maryanne?" Mark-O asks, and the answer is truthful. Thus, Mark-O in his own way is learning about the nature of death and anticipates the actuality; he senses the impending grief.

1. Virginia Lee, *The Magic Moth* (New York: Seabury Press, 1972).

As the family gathers in Maryanne's room the afternoon before she dies, the intense emotion is relieved by the sight of a white moth flying out the open window. It is the moth that emerged from Mark-O's jar holding the cocoon.

When Mark-O views Maryanne's body in a coffin, he watches his older brother and, like him, keeps from crying, but he gives full vent to tears when he's in bed. Like the rest of the family, he doesn't feel like eating or talking much, and doesn't want to go to the funeral. "I wish I could run away," he says, but he goes with the others, and, like the other children in the family, he places a rosebud on Maryanne's coffin.

For many days afterward Mark-O keeps imagining that Maryanne will reappear in her room, and he keeps asking questions. Then something happens that brings him solace and satisfaction. The seed he had planted in a pot comes up and he calls it "The Maryanne Tree." Something else occurs during this slow sad time. Remembering Maryanne and recalling the white moth, Mark-O is inspired to draw a picture—a beautiful picture of a moth. After considerable effort Mark-O succeeds, and everyone in the family admires what he's done, responding to the feeling and the symbolism. The picture makes Mark-O feel sad, and happy, too.

This wistful story, without exaggeration or morbidity, tells us (child and adult readers alike) how a child *lives* through tragedy within the family; how he slowly gains understanding of death by having his questions answered, and recovers from grief by being included in all aspects of the event; how finally he makes his own creative contribution to the memory of his sister with whom he had enjoyed a loving relationship.

A relationship with a sister or a brother, though always close in childhood, is not always loving. It is often complicated by birth order and affected by rivalry in everyday living. Thus, in the case of the death of a sibling, conflicting emotions may follow. The relationship between twins is even closer and more complicated. Therefore, the death of one produces a specially profound effect on the other.

Author Ilse-Margret Vogel gives us the poignant details of the lives of eight-year-old twins, Erika and Inge.[2] They had common interests and tastes, they both played up the similarity in their looks, they exchanged possessions, resorted to tricks to gain advantage. The advantage seemed always to be on the stronger Erika's side. Erika even flaunted the fact that she was (technically) "older." Inge, resenting the domineering Erika, is finally provoked to say, "I wish you were dead." Not long afterward, when Erika becomes ill and dies, Inge at first finds advantage in being "the only one," is pleased with establishing her own identity at last, and with the possession of extra toys. But this feeling is soon dissipated and Inge faces the stronger feeling of real loss, of missing her sister. She feels terrible remorse for having wished her sister dead and having spoken those awful words. She worries over the power of her bad thoughts and confides this to her mother; then the mother shares her own grief with Inge. When Inge is able to be helpful to her mother, and together they move Erika's bed to the attic, Inge resolves to live fully, accepting the memories and no longer being stifled by guilt and remorse.

2. Ilse-Margret Vogel, *My Twin Sister Erika* (New York: Harper & Row, 1976).

What a relief it was for Inge to spill out her "bad" thoughts about her sister to her mother and to share their mutual feelings. Life seemed worthwhile again when they could do things together afterward.

With the death of a sibling, when a child can have the comfort and love of parents with whom grief is shared, the child is supported and aided in coping with death by the presence and attention of parents, as was true of Mark-O and of Inge. It is very different, however, when a child, still young, faces the greatest loss of all, the death of a parent. There are now "nearly a half-million children affected by the crisis of parental death each year."[3]

Eda LeShan, a well-known family counselor and sensitive educator, tells children who have suffered the death of a parent how "terrible" it is.[4] She tells of the numbness, the disbelief, the fear, the anger, the confusion; and she tells it in an utterly honest and empathetic manner. Then she reminds the reader that it is important to recognize and express such feelings (though some adults may admonish a child to "be brave"), for afterward one is better able to return to activities and to other concerns. Grief cannot be arbitrarily timed, and Eda LeShan tells her readers that sadness might take a long time to run its course. She doesn't minimize the difficulty in communicating during this time, but points to the help that can come from different relatives. Especially important for a child is to be included, to be able to take part in family rituals or memorials. The author tells at the end of the book about Liz. Remembering her

3. Muriel Fischer, "Dealing with Death in the Family," *The New York Times Magazine*, March 13, 1977, p. 82.
4. Eda LeShan, *Learning to Say Good-by* (New York: Macmillan Co., 1976).

father during a memorial visit to the cemetery with family and close friends, Liz does a cartwheel on her father's grave. She had always done cartwheels with special pleasure and her father had loved to see her doing them. Now, after sadness and passivity, she is finally able to do something that comes naturally and that relates positively to the dead parent.

At one funeral service where a young child was present at her father's burial, each family member, according to their religious custom, threw a handful of earth into the grave. When the child showed her intent to do likewise, the mother feared the act would be much too upsetting to the little girl and she longed to shield her. However, profoundly sad as the act was, it gave the child a sense of membership in the group of mourners, a feeling of being a real participant in this necessary task—on a par with others. Realizing this later the mother was relieved that her youngest child too had been allowed to participate in the funeral.

When ninety-nine-year-old Great-grandmother Proctor died in 1976, the three generations of her descendants were present at her funeral. The three (of her thirteen) great-grandchildren were not merely standing still and watching the burial, but had an important contribution to make. In accordance with the plan of the oldest, each of the great-grandchildren placed a rose on the coffin, the final flowery offering to Great-grandmother Proctor. Most impressed by the funeral service and his part in it was six-year-old Carl. Later, there was a large family gathering for the purpose of an informal memorial service. Since Mrs. Proctor was close to a hundred years of age and had suffered from numerous ailments and complaints there were no expressions of profound shock or grief at this gathering. Instead, several relatives related incidents from the life of the deceased. To Carl, they were a fascinating remembrance of true stories! He, too, remembered some occasions of being with "Grammy." He, too, could get up and tell a story about Grammy and everybody would listen to him. However, Carl's grandfather divined Carl's intention in time and definitely discouraged him from carrying it out. What was questionable in the adult's mind was not the child's sincerity and good feeling, but the possible inappropriateness of a child's candid remarks. Yet, one can speculate on the just-as-possible aptness and the significance of the contribution that Carl might have made to the memorial service of his ancestor.

The death of a very old person, leaving thirteen great-grandchildren and having actually finished her life, is a natural and peaceful event and not uncommon in this era of medical advances. But neither is it uncommon in our era, in our violence-prone, civilized world, for an unnatural, untimely, and grievously tragic death to occur; a death in which a child can suddenly be deprived of not one parent, but both.

It is difficult to speak of such a tragedy even after decades have passed. It is difficult for me to write about my own parents who were murdered by anti-revolutionary, anti-Semitic bandits in a Ukrainian village during the early years of the Russian Revolution, in the twenties. The oldest of the six children in the family was my seventeen-year-old sister. She recalls now that she never talked about our parents' death. Their violent demise was such a heavy blow, her suffering so severe then, that she still feels the pain. Immediately following the tragedy she wanted to behave properly, in a brave and stoical manner. Assuming necessary family leadership, she talked with an uncle, who became our guardian, concerning practical matters. She behaved stoically and tried to be cheerful and positive with the younger children. She cried only in the night, she recalls. And now, in her seventies, whenever she senses any trouble, she remembers her parents. "But I try not to remember *all*," she says, "that's too painful . . . the wound in my soul hasn't healed, and never will."

Overwhelmed by unexpressed heavy feelings, stifled by the strain of appearing stoical, she had denied herself the natural need to mourn; denied herself the solace of talking with the younger siblings and sharing the sadness with them, or sharing the burden of grief with relatives.

I was about twelve at the time of my parents' death. My immediate and strongest feeling was *disbelief* that it had happened. For relief from grief, I clung to daytime fantasies and repeated night dreams in which my parents were still living. At that time I wished more than anything to be around my older sister whom I had always adored, but she didn't make herself available. Not being allowed to go to the funeral, I was overwhelmed with confusion and despair. I longed to see whatever tangible remains there were of my parents. I required proof that they really were dead. But my sister persuaded our uncle-guardian that it wasn't good for any children, including herself, to go to the burial and funeral; it wasn't good, she contended, to be further confronted with and thus dwell on the tragedy. I felt excluded and frustrated by not going, and I *was* still dwelling on my parents' death, my soul was still in mourning. I couldn't part with thoughts about my parents, and I did not want to part from my two younger brothers and two younger twin sisters. I wished I were joining them when my older sister placed them in a children's home. After they had left, I suffered an additional loss and felt further isolated and helpless. But since I had always tried to emulate my older sister, I *tried* to be as stoical as she during the day, though I wept copiously at night.

Gradually, I responded to the demands of housework in my uncle's home and, encouraged by my sister, to the challenge of classes in a new school. Then, a few years later, without much thinking, I agreed to join my uncle's family, and along with my six-year-old twin sisters, to emigrate to the United States.

I was soon completely absorbed with the lengthy journey, the trying detentions en route and the excitement of confronting the new world. The urgency of learning English and the need for immediate adjustment superseded the lingering sadness. Now I have warm memories of my parents' industriousness, their love, and the family life we had before their death.

Looking back on my own childhood experience it seems clear that the death of my parents was more difficult to bear, the grief made more painful, by the exclusion from the funeral, by the strenuous and vain effort to be stoical, and by not openly sharing feelings. Those months and years of unexpressed sorrow sapping youthful energy could have been spared. Yet, I survived and recovered to pursue life and work. My sister believes that being the oldest of the children she has suffered most; the rest of us, being younger, got over the grief more easily. Perhaps. The age of a child is a factor in his tolerance of grief, but not the only one.

Reading Mary McCarthy's account of her childhood which includes her being orphaned at the age of six, it is heartening to discover how resilient, resourceful, and even tough children can be after suffering the greatest loss of all—the death of parents on whom thus far they had depended completely and unquestioningly.[5]

It was during the 1918 flu epidemic that the young McCarthy parents came down with the disease while the family was traveling by train from their home in Seattle to the home of the McCarthy grandparents in Minneapolis. Both parents died there within a few days of each other. The four small children, Mary and her three younger brothers, were kept in isolation and not told of their parents' death. Mary McCarthy writes that, "Mama and Daddy, they assured us, had gone to get well in the hospital."[6] The children suffered weeks of weary waiting and painful apprehension till they came to the inevitable and silent conclusion that their parents were dead. She writes "my heart had grown numb," and though she considered herself clever to *know* the truth, she would not "speak of that knowledge or even react to it privately, for I wished to have nothing to do with it."[7]

Reconstructing this period in her life, Miss McCarthy conveys the children's hardships not only from the loss of parents but from the radical change in the children's lives. The change from a life of gaiety and paren-

5. Mary McCarthy, *Memories of a Catholic Girlhood* (New York: Harcourt, Brace & Co., 1957).
6. Ibid., p. 36.
7. Ibid., p. 38.

tal indulgence to strict discipline, oppressive righteous-
ness, and condescension created in the children a new
image of themselves: "the image, if we had guessed it, of
the orphan . . . was already forming in our minds."[8]

Through it all, the child Mary hungered for filial
love and attention, making the most of the relatives that
came through, whether the Catholic or Protestant
grandparent or the Jewish grandmother. So much of
Mary's energy was expended in putting up with innumerable restrictions and denials of being an orphan! One
can't help observing that keeping the McCarthy children in the dark about what happened to their parents
was an unnecessary hardship, adding to the severity of
their abandoned condition.

More so than adults, children *want to know* everything. For this, they are endowed with curiosity,
equipped with powers of observation, and they possess
an *un*measurable capacity for discerning details. This is
often effectively described by fiction writers.

The day after his father dies in an auto accident,
Rufus slips out of the house and discusses the technical
points of the accident, with attention to the exact posi-
tion and condition of the automobile; he recognizes all
the while the *newsworthiness* of the event and his own
enviable status related to such news! He is struggling to
find out and to understand all the aspects, as well as the
side effects and related acts, of the death of his father.
He senses acutely the sudden stillness with which the
corpse is viewed by all; he feels the frightful finality in
the prescribed composure of the dead. This is what
Rufus notices about his dead father:

8. Ibid., p. 36.

The arm was bent. Out of the dark suit, the starched cuff, sprang the hairy wrist.

The wrist was angled; the hand was arched; none of the fingers touched each other.

The hand was so composed that it seemed at once casual and majestic. It stood exactly above the center of his body.

The fingers looked unusually clean and dry, as if they had been scrubbed with great care.

The hand looked very strong, and the veins were strong in it.

The nostrils were very dark, yet he thought he could see in one of them, something which looked like cotton. . . .

The hair was most carefully brushed.

The eyes were casually and quietly closed, the eyelids were like silk on the balls, and when Rufus glanced quickly from the eyes to the mouth it seemed as if his father were almost about to smile. Yet the mouth carried no suggestion either of smiling or of gravity; only strength, silence, manhood, and indifferent contentment.

He saw him much more clearly than he had ever seen him before; yet his face looked unreal, as if he had just been shaved by a barber. The whole head was waxen, and the hand, too, was as if perfectly made of wax.

The head was lifted on a small white satin pillow.

There was the subtle, curious odor, like fresh hay, and like a hospital, but not quite like either, and so faint that it was scarcely possible to be sure that it existed.[9]

Rufus was not merely viewing the corpse, but with all his senses raised to their highest acuity was absorbing

9. James Agee, "A Death in the Family," in *A Reader for Parents,* selected by the Child Study Association (New York: W. W. Norton, 1963), p. 440.

everything related to his father's death, in the process of coming to terms with it.

Seeing a loved relative no longer alive is shocking and horrifying, but children can live through these painful reactions and overcome the hurt. However, when children are not allowed to see the dead or to know exactly what happens to the body after death they are apt to imagine a more frightening sight than the reality of a corpse and the irrevocable act of burial.

Eda LeShan tells of the tortuous experience that seven-year-old Allen went through—which could have been avoided.[10]

Allen knew about and waited for the addition of a baby to his family, his home. But the birth that took place at the hospital was premature; the infant died a few hours later and was cremated without a funeral. On returning from the hospital the parents did tell Allen that the baby had been born too small and too weak to live. After hearing the news, Allen *wanted to know* what they did with the baby and where it actually was, but he was "too shy to ask." Perhaps he even sensed that his mother would be reluctant to answer him. Subsequently, Allen developed strong fears of many things, including the fear of opening closet doors and drawers. When a psychologist was consulted, Allen revealed his imagining that the dead baby was somewhere in the house and that he might inadvertently discover it. This would be too awful to happen. With the help of the psychologist, and with honest communication with his parents, Allen soon overcame his fears.

Clearly, it was necessary for Allen's mental health to

10. LeShan, *Learning to Say Good Good-by,* pp. 14–16.

know what his parents had done with the baby and where it actually was. Thus, allowing children to go to a funeral may seem to adults inappropriate, yet it proves to be of positive value to children. The little girl throwing a handful of earth into her father's grave, Carl placing a rose on the coffin, each feels the importance of the occasion and a personal respect for the dead.

Not knowing the facts of death, or misconstruing the meaning of overheard common terms pertaining to death, children sometimes arrive at serious misconceptions. Four-year-old Ivan overheard his mother saying on the telephone that Mr. Peterson's "body" was being flown in from overseas. Since *his* use of the word "body" related only to a living person, with head *and* body, he listened wide-eyed and asked uncomprehendingly, "But what did they do with Mr. Peterson's *head?*" When his mother explained to Ivan that "body" meant Mr. Peterson was flown in dead, not decapitated, more confusion resulted. Learning that his father was making arrangements for a flight out of town, Ivan became panicky: he was now linking airplanes with death. Again his mother explained to Ivan that flying was not the cause of death, but simply a means of transportation.

Learning of a child's experience with the death of parents in a distant country and a different culture enlarges our comprehension of life and strengthens our universal human ties. Pearl Buck, in her realistic style, tells us about a natural disaster, a tidal wave that destroys a small Japanese fishing village.[11] A young boy, Jiya, is saved by his friend Kino's family, farmers who live above the raging waters. But Jiya's home and both

11. Pearl S. Buck, *The Big Wave* (New York: John Day, 1948).

his parents are swept away and swallowed by the sea.

In his wisdom, and in keeping with Japanese tradition, Kino's father gently assumes a paternal role toward Jiya. He advises the rest of the family to leave Jiya to mourn in his own passive way, accepting the naturalness of Jiya's ample tears. The older man doesn't urge Jiya to eat and to play till Jiya is ready. When the boy starts eating, Kino's father knows that Jiya's body is recovering "and would heal the mind and the soul."

Gradually Jiya responds to the welcoming family, to his friend Kino's activities, and especially to the lively little sister. After that Jiya regains his zest for life.

Here, in a traditional Japanese setting, a grieving child without relatives is welcomed and comforted by a genuinely friendly family; with them he is free to express his grief over the death of his parents, and to take the time he needs for his sadness to run its course.

In our society, a child grieving from death in the family who does not have immediate relatives or close friends or, simply, sufficient communication at home may find help in his school. Certainly not in every case, but it does happen that a child can receive understanding and comfort from talking to a teacher or a counselor in school. The importance to a grieving child of a sympathetic, listening teacher is pointed out in an article by Louise Bates Ames.[12]

In our relatively young, multicultural, and fast-changing country, many people do not live or die surrounded by traditions. An individual family may regu-

12. Louise Bates Ames, "Death: Ways to Help Children Get Perspective," *The Instructor,* January 1969.

late burials and memorials and the extent of children's participation in attention to the dead in its own way.

In caring for an aged, dying family member some independent Americans follow their own convictions, contrary to the usual practices in their community. Such a situation is described in an unusual documentary book. Instead of institutionalizing a senile, dying man, the entire family accepts his presence at home and accommodates to his needs. The man's wife, daughter, the two grandsons, a granddaughter-in-law and a young great-granddaughter, Hillary, all share in the care of Gramp. Although Gramp responds to the nursing care that stretches over a couple of years, he prudently and deliberately gives up his burdensome living and dies. As though saying, "enough of this nonsense," he removes his false teeth and announces that he will no longer eat or drink. He keeps his word—and his action is respected by the family—and three weeks later he dies. All this is reported with candor and artistry, documented with written records, taped comments, and photographs by the two grandsons.[13]

This "documentary" presents the involvement of all the family members in the needed care of Gramp, including casual attention to unpleasant chores when he is incontinent, and in putting up with the idiosyncrasies and absurdities of senility. He is accepted at the table even when he is not fit company—he passes his dentures to be buttered! The three-year-old Hillary* is interested in all the facts, and seems to understand what's going on with Gramp as well as anyone else. Watching her

---

*She was five at the time Gramp died.

13. Mark Jury and Dan Jury, *Gramp* (New York: Grossman, 1976).

mother's toileting attention to Gramp, she observes, "He's so old he forgot how to do it himself." She holds his hands and finds him lovable. The authors tell us that:

> In the months following Gramp's death, we kept a wary eye on Hillary, wondering if the experience had caused her any harm. But today she shows a tolerance and acceptance of aging and death that are enviable to any who had such matters treated as mysterious and forbidden during their own childhood.
>
> What Hillary does remember and speak of quite often are the characters that Gramp introduced to us—the chillysmiths, rupes, Michigans, and bugeyes.
>
> "Why do you remember those imaginary characters so vividly?" I asked her one day.
>
> "They are not imaginary," she retorted with conviction. "They're real. They're not pretend.
>
> "They moved over to our house," she confided to me in conspiratorial tones, "they tied strings together and made themselves into a mobile in my room. They look like fish now. They remind me of Gramp."[14]

In her firsthand experience with senility and death at home, Hillary not only showed realism and toughness, but she was able to react with characteristic childish (and charming) imagination, giving her perhaps an advantage over the adults.

Three to five is an age when a child may become aware of death even without an actual experience and may startle an adult with questions "out of the blue." When my daughter was four she startled me by asking,

14. Ibid., pp. 151–52.

for no apparent reason, "When are you going to die, Mother?" Regaining my composure I answered, "I suppose when I am quite old." "But who'll take care of me then?" she asked with a note of worry in her voice this time. "Well! You'll be old enough to take care of yourself then!" I answered, feeling relieved. And her reaction to that was expressed in one telling syllable: "Oh!"

No further words were necessary. The implication in the "Oh!" was clear enough—all that mattered to her was the assurance of being cared for. Her initial question may have *seemed* callous—as it would be if asked by a calculating adult, greedy for an inheritance—but for a four-year-old it was a natural, even a necessary, egocentric concern.

In order to understand children's reactions to death in the family and be able to offer helpful guidance, we try (by talking) to discern the child's level of understanding and misunderstanding about death; to sense the child's fears of death and defenses against it.

Four-year-old George learned that when people get old they eventually die. He later talked about age with his father who readily, and jokingly, admitted to "getting on in years." On his father's birthday shortly afterward, George insisted that his father be twenty years younger. "Why," asked the mother, "should Daddy be only twenty years old?" "So he wouldn't die so soon," the little boy answered seriously.

Such desire to delay aging for the parent and to postpone indefinitely the time of death is a natural defense. We recognize the comfort it brings—to us as well as to children.

Kornei Chukovsky (the late Russian children's poet and well-known authority on the young child) believed that "optimism is as essential to the child as the air he breathes," and that knowledge of death is too harsh a blow to endure.[15] For this reason young children are tireless and most ingenious in their seeking to protect themselves and their loved ones from death. Chukovsky illustrates his belief with children's own words.

A round-eyed boy, about four and a half, looked out of the bus window at a funeral procession and said, with serenity: "Everyone will die, but I'll remain."

"Mother," said four-year-old Anka, "all the people will die. But someone will have to place somewhere the urn with the ashes of the last dead person. Let me do it! All right?"

Touching, varied, and shrewd are the many ways in which the child drives the thought of his death out of mind. Recreating optimism is one of the great laws of the child's life.[16]

Alik Babenisher thought of a good way to postpone the death of his mother:

"Mommie, now I know everything! You'll eat yogurt both in the morning and in the evening, and I'll not eat it at all. That way we'll both die at the same time."

This little boy had listened to a lecture on "Longevity" on a radio program, which stressed the beneficial role of yogurt in assuring good health and longevity.

And the following about Alenushka:

She tried to persuade us and her grandmother not to die until she was grown up and would find a medicine

15. Kornei Chukovsky, *From Two to Five*, trans. Miriam Morton (Berkeley: University of California Press, 1963), p. 46.
16. Ibid., p. 47.

against old age and death. "Because there must not be any death."[17]

The Russian children whom Chukovsky quotes, as well as Annie, the Navajo child, and George, and the nursery-school children (in chapter 2), all rejected what they were not able to cope with. Many children reject their own death or that of their loved ones. Sylvia Anthony concludes from her extensive studies that only when a child manifests extreme anxiety does the adult need to go along with a child's vehement denial and say, "You need never die," in order for such a child to gather strength and respond positively to his environment and be ready *later* to come to terms with the truth about death. Thus, "some temporary denial of reality may have positive value in relieving anxiety and permitting subsequent acceptance."[18]

Chukovsky, however, believed that we must temporarily save all children from the truth and protect them from sorrow by feeding their optimism on illusions, by deliberately concealing facts, by going along with children's optimistic pretending. Modern psychological findings indicate that, while one should recognize the need for protection against grief and fear of death, it is important to be truthful with children, even preschoolers, about the facts of death as they come up, and about the feelings of sorrow from loss that need to be expressed. This builds a healthy, trusting relationship between children and adults, gives personal knowledge of significant events in the children's lives, and corrects harmful misconceptions. Furthermore, adults

17. Ibid., p. 50.
18. Sylvia Anthony, *The Discovery of Death in Childhood and After* (Middlesex, Eng.: Penguin Books, 1973), p. 163.

themselves need to examine their own attitudes toward death for "acknowledging the reality of death is an essential component of a mature personality."[19] We do not deny children protection, but we do not confuse them by explaining death with euphemisms,, such as "going to sleep" or "going away."[20] We respond to children's need to know about death and respect their strength and humanity as well as their immaturity.

In spite of the long-held taboo about public discussion of death or inclusion of the theme in the education of children, the subject has always been important to parents.

Here is my own record from the early fifties.

When at the meeting the subject of death was brought up by one parent, the others were concerned about giving children the right ideas on the subject, yet shielding them from unnecessary shock. There was an agreement among the parents that children must be told what happened since, as one mother put it, "You can't *hide* anything from them anyway." The following recent experience was related.

With the death of grandfather who lived near by and whom Mary, four-and-a-half, knew intimately, the grieving mother was at first at a great loss as to what to tell the child. How much to give of the awful facts, and how much to reveal of her own deep feelings. But when the expressive child asked with genuine concern quite simple questions, the mother answered truthfully. She found that it didn't make the child panicky; instead, it made her

19. Dixie R. Crase and Darrel Crase, "Helping Children Understand Death," *Young Children,* November 1976.
20. Daniel Goleman, "We Are Breaking the Silence about Death," *Psychology Today,* September 1976.

thoughtful and reflective and sad. When Mary said to her mother: "This is the saddest day in my life," the mother was not only moved by the child's expression of grief, of deep feeling, but she felt comforted herself by what she and her little girl now *shared.*

Even the "saddest day" can be endured by children when the experience and suffering are shared. But when parents keep knowledge of death from children and deny them participation in funeral procedures the children will feel isolated and burdened by confusion and by unexpressed grief. Communicating the truth to children, fact and feeling, when death in the family occurs, encouraging their expressions of grief, and bringing children in on whatever religious, spiritual, or ethnic form of funeral are important in developing family feeling and respect for traditions. The personal experience with death can add to the strength and spirit in one's own life.

6

"CAN YOU STILL HAVE A BIRTHDAY WHEN YOU DIE?"

Remembering and Celebrating Those Who Died

Wherever we turn we encounter reminders of the lives of people no longer physically among us. We engage in celebrations of historical events, preservation of landmark buildings, observance of holidays honoring great persons from the past, reliving traditions dating centuries back. All these are brought to children's attention at home, in school, and in general living as a matter of course, with focus on the immediate festivity and involvement. We have dinner on Thanksgiving, give presents for Christmas, light candles for Chanukah, enjoy a school holiday on Lincoln's birthday. Not much attention is necessarily given to our connection to the past. Yet, historical objects and symbols teach us the value of an important life of the past which we live with and honor in the present. But how much history do children understand or are interested in?

For children of preschool and early school age, history as a subject is remote and impersonal, though they may recite historical names and events. However, there is understandable drama and appealing heroism to children in great names that they hear about, names of people who died long ago.

When one is attuned to catching children's spontaneous conversations, one can discern "historical comments," in the following, made in passing, by five-year-olds.

> ". . . Lincoln died.
> "He was shot—by a soldier."
>
> "God doesn't die ever."
> "Oh, yes, He died once, and came to life again."
> "Jesus was nailed on a cross and He looked horrible with blood coming out."[1]

No addition to the comments or lesson was made (or needed to be made) by the listening adult.

Young children can also become imaginatively involved with a historical figure. Watch four-and-a-half-year-old Freddie (a German refugee child).

> The day after Lincoln's birthday Freddie came to school with an announcement: "I am Lincoln." He poked with his foot in the snow a while, then picked up a stick and began digging in the snow with it, saying, "I am Lincoln. Lincoln is working now."
> In due course the stick-shovel became a stick-gun. Freddie put the gun across his shoulder and began

1. Cohen and Rudolph, *Kindergarten and Early Schooling,* p. 72.

marching with it, saying, "I am Lincoln. Lincoln is a sol-
dier." All his movements were simple and clear and inte-
grated with his thoughts. There was seriousness in his face
but there were lightness and change in it too.

When the soldiering was done with, the "gun" was
transformed into a "banner." Gaily now Freddie carried it
in front of him singing softly, "Happy Birthday." The air
of festivity and pleasure emanating from Freddie made
the other children join him. They all sang "Happy Birthday, dear Lincoln."

An hour later inside the large nursery school room a
teacher was at the piano with the children gathered about
her. They were whispering and hesitating with their re-
quests for songs. Then came Freddie's request: "I want to
sing happy birthday, happy birthday to Lincoln." And
they all sang it.

The Lincoln idea grew as the day progressed. Before
settling down for a nap, Freddie warned: "Don't call me
Freddie. No. My name is Lincoln. Abraham Lincoln."

When everything became quiet in the sleeping room,
Freddie lifted his head and confided in an audible
whisper, "Lincoln was a very good man. I am Abraham
Lincoln."[2]

We see how meaningful the life of a historical person can be, even for a young child, and how deeply,
through free play, the child can identify with a hero!

If along with or after such play a question about *what
happens* when people die should come up, the answers
from the adult or from children themselves could be to
this effect: dead people are buried, but not forgotten;
those who loved them are sad and show it, and then

2. Marguerita Rudolph, "Identification through Finding a Hero," *Childhood Education,* May 1949.

attend to their own lives; mainly, people who die are remembered in different ways.

Hearing of the school holiday in celebration of Lincoln's birthday a little girl comments reflectively: "When you die—can you still have a Birth Day (party)?" Was she actually thinking: does a person revive after death to attend a birthday celebration? Or did she realize that a birthday can be celebrated by relatives and friends in memory of the dead who cannot be physically present? It's difficult to know exactly what the little girl meant, but the answer should be in terms of *remembering* someone who died and observing a birthday *for* that someone.

Recently there was a celebration of Beethoven's birthday by a third-grade class in a city public school.[3] The celebration was organized and led by members of a musical society and the school's music teacher. The 33 children, aged seven to eight, did not have special musical training or knowledge of Beethoven's music. The event was intended to commemorate the composer's 206th birthday with an "ordinary" public school class. Selections of Beethoven's music were played by musicians, and there was singing and humming by all.

A birthday celebration naturally requires a cake, and the cake in this instance was inscribed with chocolate musical notes and the words to go with them from the Ninth Symphony: "Alle Menschen werden Brüder." The children were seated on the floor listening and watching while Beethoven's music was played and the cake was being cut. Surely, each child must have been eager for his or her piece. Yet, before anyone was given

3. Barbara Campbell, *The New York Times,* December 17, 1976.

a portion, one boy said: "Give the first piece to Bee-thoven." What a genuine, generous, and truly childlike way to honor someone—with a "first piece of birthday cake!" The children also heard about Beethoven's struggle with his deafness and his strong belief in brotherhood. The celebration ended with the music teacher playing "Ode to Joy" while children hummed along.

How warmly and personally those children (from a regular, not a music, class) responded to the lively memorial!

Since so much of our music has been composed by musicians no longer living, music education can bring children naturally to memorializing or gaining aware-ness of someone dead yet meaningful in our lives.

On a recent national TV program *(Today)* the pianist Lorin Hollander told of playing informally for children in Harlem, telling them whose music he played. After he played a piece by Schubert a seven-year-old child asked him: "Isn't he dead?" "Yes," Hollander answered, "but he left his music to us." "But how do you know what he *means?*" the child probed further. Hollander perceived in the question the child's concern that the music be played in accordance with the dead composer's wishes and intent. Such response from a child was in-spiring to the adult musician, causing him to be more aware of interpreting faithfully a composer's "mean-ing."

Children of all ages are aware of important visible objects in their environment. The George Washington Bridge is impressive in its construction and span, its function, its durability, and the significant name re-membered for centuries. John F. Kennedy International Airport, a colossal station for air travelers of the world, is impressive as an edifice suddenly *re*named in memory of a president who was a national hero. A Martin Luther King, Jr., public school, accommodating hundreds or thousands of children and adults, and displaying prominently the portrait of the man, is impressive because it is *named* for a universally admired social leader who worked to overcome discrimination and died a violent death.

The significance of naming a structure is not lost on children and helps them be aware that a life is not always obliterated by death.

Buildings named for great leaders, scientists, or artists and statues and portraits of them hung in public places can be easily observed, inspected, read, and talked about. But the most natural and relevant occasion to talk about the death of an important person is at the time of its occurrence. This is history on the spot. Because of the prevalence of violence in modern times, overt assassination and covert killings of national leaders are, regrettably, not uncommon. And owing to the efficiency of the modern news media, children of all ages become quickly aware of such shocking, tragic news. They become conversant with the details of the death as well as the historical significance of the event and the character of the victim.

When President John F. Kennedy was assassinated, a group of social scientists (psychologists, psychiatrists, educators) made a broad study of children's reactions to the event.[4] Aided by the full exposure on television, the

---

4. Martha Wolfenstein and Gilbert Kliman, eds., *Children and the Death of a President* (Garden City, N.Y.: Doubleday Anchor, 1966).

tragedy made as great an impact on children (young and middle school age) as it did on adults. The study showed that among the children studied there was initially a universal expression of disbelief—it can't be true. Shock and numbness and disinterest in usual activities were also commonly expressed. The most disturbing aspect of the assassination to the children seemed to be that the father of young children had died.

From the results of the questionnaires and interviews, and from the children's own writing, the scientists noted that children under the age of twelve have a short span of enduring grief (compared to adults), and that they need and usually seek distraction (they can even joke about the event); and they resort to various defenses against grief. A nine-year-old girl told in an interview how *unbearable* it would be if you couldn't *forget* grief. They also noted that American children have difficulty in expressing feelings when speaking; but it's different with writing—writing does provide a better medium for expression of strong feelings. One explanation of the abundant expression of concern and sadness on this occasion is that it is easier to "mourn at a distance"—express grief for someone who is distant from one's actual life, not a close relation or someone you know.

In the study, children of all ages, but especially boys, showed inhibition about crying in public. And many children praised Mrs. Kennedy highly for being so "brave" and not crying at the funeral.

It is not suggested here that parents and teachers should pounce on a national disaster in order to take advantage of it for the sake of education about death. Rather, caring adults can share with children knowledge and feelings about the event, and not only allow but encourage expression of normal curiosity, as well as humane concern about the end of a life. Such sharing would actually constitute education about death and may, in a way, serve as preparation for a personal encounter with death.

When the great American artist, Alexander Calder, died suddenly in December of 1976, on a trip to New York City to oversee a highly acclaimed exhibition of his work, the news made a special impression on a class of fourth graders in a New York public school. Only a week before, the class had gone with their teacher to see the exhibition. Since then the children had been making wire sculptures, playful mobiles, pen-and-ink drawings with spots—trying out a Calder kind of art.

Because of his fame, Calder's death made front-page and TV news, so the children talked about it the next day. They talked about his being an old man in his seventies (therefore death was to be expected); about his continued work throughout his life. The children became aware that the artist's death brought a new appreciation of all his existing works. It brought a realization that recognized art, such as Calder's, lives on: it is treasured, protected, exhibited, loved by, and inspiring to, generations of people. Since I myself own a minor Calder creation (a wire buckle) I, too, felt after the artist's death that the buckle was an heirloom to be passed on.

The fourth-grade children expressed sadness that Calder's creative life had now stopped. While talking with the teacher they commented on the artist's family, and the teacher then suggested writing condolence letters to Calder's widow, Louisa Calder. Though none of the children had written condolence letters before, their

familiarity with Calder's works and their feeling about
the artist as a person provided an occasion for such
thoughtful activity. Here are two of the letters, unedited
by any adult:

Dear Mrs. Calder,
I'm very sorry to here about what happened to Mr. Calder. We liked the work that he did. When we grow up we
want to be artists. We had wished Mr. Calder could come
to P.S. 75 and give Miss Lowy's class a lesson in art. Some
of the things that we liked best were his toys, stabiles,
mobiles, circus, paintings, and wire sculptures. We did
some wire sculptures and paintings like his because our
class is making a Jr. Calder exhibit and because we liked
his things very much. This is one of the paintings we
made.
Sincerely yours,
Amy and Laurie, Room 102
P.S. Please write back.

Nov. 16, 1976
Dear Mrs. Calder,
Our class went to the whitney museum to look at Mr.
Calder's work. We saw the clock, and lots of more. When
we heard about Mr. Calder was dead at 10:00 AM, we
talked about it. And we made a exhibit called . . . THE
JUNIOR CALDER EXHIBIT. We made lots of things
like . . . Cars, People, Guns, Clocks, Scopes and MUCH!
MUCH MORE!
SINCERELY THOMAS

The reader will notice how direct and specific the
letters are about Calder's art and his death. Clearly, the
children are praising the artist Calder, yet full of importance of their own activity, *their* Jr. Calder exhibit.

Condolence letters are not pleasant or easy for children or adults to write. The task requires confrontation with the event of death, it elicits respect or deference toward the deceased and recognition of the loss to the relatives. Naturally, condolence letters are not often of a literary caliber, but they are a personal expression of sympathy for anyone writing them. For children, offering sympathy to the bereaved is an unusual act of benevolence, as well as an experience in understanding the meaning of death.

Their own family history is of tremendous personal interest to children. A preschooler who has only vague notions of his own past is nevertheless fascinated by his remote babyhood. "What was I like *before* I was even one year old? Tell me about . . . None years old!" six-year-old Alice begs, looking at her baby picture with superior amusement. "Were you once a little girl like me? Who was your mommy?"

It's a struggle for young children to visualize the family as different from the way it is here and now. The exact relation of the present living family members beyond the parents and the siblings—such as aunts, uncles, cousins, and even grandparents—seems too removed (or abstract) to comprehend fully. A very bright seven-year-old felt compelled to share his newfound knowledge: "You know! My *grand*mother is my father's *mother. I know that!*" The grandmother lived nearby and was a frequent visitor.

The relationship of family members no longer living is even more difficult for young children to understand. Yet, pictures and stories and family anecdotes told repeatedly when requested build up a picture of family history and make an important lasting impression on a child. In one family the three children (the youngest of whom was barely of school age) worked together to produce a family scrapbook as a present for their father a few months before his death. The scrapbook included not only family photographs of special occasions and seasons in the country, but also a running text and other memorabilia. The scrapbook took on special meaning after the father's death, and it proved to be a most read book and a treasured item for the children in years to come.

The only possession I have from my own childhood home is a linen tablecloth that had been woven and embroidered by my mother. It is a work of art, with the artist's initials and date in clear design. It must have been part of her trousseau, for the date, "1901," was the year of my mother's marriage at the age of seventeen. Although I do not remember eating off that tablecloth I recall vividly seeing it hung periodically on the fence for airing, then being returned to the mothproof chest. One item passed on in the family is thus a tangible, telling record of the industry and beauty of a life.

Oral and pictorial family history may answer important questions as the child matures. "Who am I?" "From whom do I come?" Alex Haley, an American author of the best-selling book *Roots,* was so impressed by family references to an ancestral name during his childhood that to discover who he really came from became his life's chief challenge.[5] The result of his dedicated and painful search led at long last to the discovery of his original name and to his African ancestor who became an American slave. This proved to be not only of value

5. Alex Haley, *Roots* (Garden City, N.Y.: Doubleday & Co., 1976).

to Alex Haley, but of interest to millions of others who read his book and watched the TV dramatization. Haley's great-grandchildren will surely know *their* roots, and honor their ancestors.

By gradually grasping the nature of kinship and the role of ancestors, children recognize the importance of names. A name is synonymous with self, gives one uniqueness. When children first learn to write, they tirelessly write their own name over and over again on any possible surface! And a name is often a family history. Although modern American children may be named for their parents' friends or some whimsical or literary character, many children in countries throughout the world are named for relatives, living or dead. Passing on of names is a significant connection that a child may not be aware of, but find fascinating when it is brought to his attention. In Russia, where people are known by their patronymics (father's first name, next to one's own name), a person has a lifetime connection with his father. Thus children always know their grandfathers' names by knowing their parents'. In the Jewish tradition, children are named for dead relatives, with direct ancestors having a priority. Thus, a sense of family is strengthened and a child's feeling of belonging is established or clarified.

A family tree is an impressive and graphic presentation of names in the generations and branches of the family. For people who have genealogical records of names and dates, a family tree is a truly historical family treasure to be passed on. However, for those of us without sufficient records, even a small family tree, with missing branches, can be constructed as a family project involving the children. Such a project would give historical meaning to the children's own names and develop personal concepts of ancestors and descendants, involving the passing on of names in the generations.

Besides the passing on of names in the family, there is the universal act of passing on other tangibles of greater or lesser worth which allows children to remember relatives who have died. Family homes, farms, furniture, jewelry, clothing may have been passed on through several generations and be in current use. Children are quick to see the benefit of obtaining something without effort when a relative dies. Chukovsky quotes a preschool child:

> "Granny, will you die?"
> "Yes, I'll die."
> "Will they bury you in a hole?"
> "Yes, they will bury me."
> "Deep?"
> "Deep."
> "Then that's when I'll be able to use your sewing machine."[6]

A thoroughly practical approach! Not wanting granny to die; simply an interest in *using* something no longer useful to granny. Still, that question about a "deep" hole. Is the depth an assurance that granny isn't going to climb out to *claim* the sewing machine? Who knows after all what the dead are capable of?

Five-year-old Jennie always admired her father's watch and one day she asked him where he got it. Her father told Jennie that he "inherited" it from *his* father who died before Jennie was born. "Inherited?" Yes,

---

6. Kornei Chukovsky, *From Two to Five*, p. 2.

when people die they leave their valuables to their children or relatives or friends, the father explained: he had inherited the watch because his father, before he died, knew how much his son (Jennie's father) liked it. Jennie caught on to the idea and applied it to a personal interest of her own. Jennie loved her aunt's clangy necklace, and her aunt let her try it on a few times. Jennie would have really liked to *have* the necklace, but at her age she knew it would not be proper to ask for it when her aunt was wearing it herself. But "inheriting" the necklace was different. When she saw her aunt again Jennie came right to the point:

"When you die, Aunt Linda, and I hope it's going to be soon, can I then have your necklace?" Jennie wasn't as patient as the Russian child (who wasn't hurrying granny's demise) but equally practical. Jennie's parents and aunt were at first shocked, then amused, by Jennie's blunt and unusual request, but then the aunt stated that she had no intention of dying, and no desire to part with the necklace. She also told Jennie that there are ways of getting what you want other than waiting for someone to die. She would, she said, buy Jennie a special necklace for her birthday next month.

It is easy to recognize in Jennie's candid request the common enough adult attitude of greed toward inheriting property as expediently as possible. We can hope that Jennie, having expressed her feelings to caring adults, learned early that one doesn't wait for a person to die; that instead one can benefit from association while the person is living.

However, when a relative dies and the family actually becomes a beneficiary according to the written will of the deceased, it is interesting and significant for the children to be told about it and to be included realistically in the benefits. A child learning that a person, in anticipation of death, can caringly provide for the surviving kin, can't help but sense the closeness of family ties and the tangible generosity of a relative. That relative, in death, can command special acknowledgment from an appreciative child. Abigail, who had only recently learned to read, managed to read in full her father's obituaries, noting of course her own name mentioned in print. This was meaningful and valuable to her as a record of her father. Equally meaningful was the knowledge of her father's will. Her questions and comments about the will showed her feeling for her father's *concern* in providing for the family after his own death.

There is another kind of tangible inheritance, though perhaps not obvious to children. It is the inheritance of special abilities: musical talent, mathematical aptitude, artistic ability perhaps, or particular external features such as red hair, brown skin. Without getting into a scientific discussion of genetics, it is important to indicate to children that such inheritance, though real enough, doesn't have a clear-cut predictability! Not *all* the progency of a musician are musical—some may even be tone-deaf. Neither is there assurance that a girl with an inherited mathematical gift, apparent at eight years of age, will also have the educational opportunity, encouragement from family, and perseverance to make full *use* of the inheritance. Nor can a boy with inherited artistic talent and a love of painting be assured of receiving necessary recognition. The boy's parents may be disappointed that the boy isn't inclined to become a lawyer, thereby earning more money. Thus, the boy's promise of becoming an artist in accordance with biological inheritance may never be realized. Clearly, a dead relative may have left you his or her talent, but couldn't possibly have left you all the conditions necessary to develop that talent.

Thus questions of who my long dead ancestors were, what traits or talents they might have passed on to me to live with, and what I may become, if answered, could serve as a *guide* to "How should I *live* before I die? What will I pass on?" as well as provide an answer to: "Can you still have a birthday when you die?"

Participating in memorialization or in observing holidays and birthdays of significant national or international figures no longer living provides an occasion for children to get a historical perspective of the dead. It affords an opportunity for children and adults for reflection on the value of a human life, and on the value of one's own (temporal) life. Learning about the sources and roots of one's family helps a child to relate better to the family and strengthens a sense of self.

7

"THERE IS ALWAYS A STARTING, AND THERE IS ALWAYS AN ENDING"

"There is always a starting, and there is always an ending," my grandson Noel said, in a contemplative mood, when he was six years old. Impressed, I urged him on.

"Like what?" I asked. He looked thoughtful, without replying. "You mean like in a story?"

"Yes," he then promptly replied. "It happens in a story," and added, "it happens with people: in starting they are born, at the end they die." He punctuated the sentence with a sigh, and was still thinking. Curious as to *what* Noel would consider next in importance to people in his universal scheme, I asked, "What else?"

"And with *cars*," the modern six-year-old answered, and continued, "the cars start getting made and end with breaking down." Then he became frivolous as he added the final segment. "And an apple at the start is fresh. But when you forget it, it ends *rotten*." The last word was said with a sense of the ultimate (no place to go beyond "rotten"). The word was clearly final and funny, and Noel laughed, repeating it with satisfaction as I wrote down what he had said.

There is always a starting,
And there is always an ending.

It happens in a story.
It happens with people:
      In starting they are born,
      At the end they die.
And with cars:
      The cars start getting made
      And end with breaking down.

And an apple at the start is fresh.
But when you forget it—
      It ends ROTTEN.

Thoughts or notions of death, concepts or misconceptions of death, are not infrequently reflected in young children's conversations, in play, and in various activities. Social scientists studying children have made extensive records and studies of children's understanding of and reaction to death at different ages and stages of development.[1] There are also master's theses (available in college libraries) that deal with the subject,[2] and no doubt more will be appearing at various universities.

Living and working with children at home, in school, or during informal encounters it is possible for any adult, without being a social scientist, to hear or overhear what children think and say with reference to death. We have seen this in situations in the earlier chapters.

1. Isaacs, *Intellectual Growth in Young Children;* Anthony, *The Discovery of Death in Childhood and After;* Marjorie Editha Mitchell, *The Child's Attitude to Death* (New York: Schocken Books, 1967).
2. Ann Watt, "Helping Children to Mourn" (New York: Bank Street College of Education, 1971); Marjory Morrow, "Death in Children's Literature" (New York: Bank Street College of Education, 1975).

Before children are old enough to be familiar with the term or have any concept of death (at about the age of two), they already have some notions of *here and not here*, of having and losing, holding and dropping, appearing and disappearing. When a child begins to talk, among the first early phrases that all parents are familiar with are, "all gone!" "no more," and of course "bye-bye." This is the beginning of the child's experience with change of condition, experience of parting with objects, or with persons. The universal game of peekaboo which, as all parents know, babies delight in playing, is in a way an exercise in disappearing and reappearing.[3] Covered up and not seeing or seen, there is a breathless moment of not being.

The conclusion from various studies relating to children's understanding of death is that until a child is approximately seven to nine he cannot be expected to understand the full meaning of death. Three-year-old Roger's asking "Who deaded the frog?" (chapter 4) is characteristic of young children's thinking that death is externally caused. The children who suggested giving food and water to the dead gerbil (chapter 4) are also expressing a concept appropriate to their age; a concept that death is reversible. Susan Isaacs cites several examples of children trying to revive dead animals by placing them in water.[4]

Piaget found that children go through stages of distinguishing what's alive from what's dead.[5] At an early stage a child regards anything that moves, including in-

3. Dixie R. Crase and Darrell Crase, "Helping Children Understand Death."
4. Isaacs, *Intellectual Growth in Young Children*, p. 182.
5. Anthony, *The Discovery of Death in Childhood and After*, p. 57.

animate objects, as alive; and anything immobile is dead. Immobility is a necessary condition when preschool children play dead! Later a child regards as alive anything mobile that is self-propelled, rather than propelled by someone else or mechanically. When children are still developing an understanding of "alive" and "dead" they are apt to become confused by the semantics of an adult's use of "live" and "dead," such as "live coal," "live wire," "dead end," "catching your death of cold," etc.

Another source of confusion about the meaning of death for some children, according to Sylvia Anthony, are mechanical toys that behave as though they were "live."[6]

A child who is still struggling to distinguish animate from inanimate objects, live from dead, can be deceived by an eye-closing, wetting doll, or a stuffed bear that produces a sound through a concealed button. This is of course different from a child *himself* endowing a stick horse or simple dolls and toy animals (without concealed mechanisms) with live attributes for which the child uses his own level of imagination and experience.

Still another confusion may result from various euphemisms for death, such as the common but vague "passed away"; or reference to the relatives of the dead person as having "lost" him or her.

I remember, a number of years ago, a middle-aged New England lady told me in a letter, "We lost our Eddie," referring to her husband. And I (not as familiar with idiomatic English as one who acquires it in childhood) assumed that her husband was actually lost on

6. Ibid., p. 59.

one of his hunting trips. I didn't learn the fact of his death till much later. This experience made me sensitive to children's possible misunderstanding of adults' common expressions. Whenever children ask me about my own parents, I never say I "lost them" at an early age, but say "they have been dead a long time." If the situation calls for it (the children look disappointed or sad), I might add: "I remember my parents, and I know what they did when they lived."

When answering children's questions about death, adults not infrequently say to children that death is *similar* to sleep or that it is a kind of sleep. It is easy to see how such a statement from an adult, especially an "all knowing" parent, would confuse the child. In some cases, psychiatrists report, such equating of death with sleep instills fear in the child or resistance to sleep that requires professional help to overcome. We can see that, although telling children that death is like sleep is an easy way out of answering a difficult question, children do need honest and more thoughtful explanations.

Since the concept of time is as complicated for children to grasp as the concept of death, uncertainty and distress may arise with the departure of close family members, especially mother. Recognizing this, many a parent has at one time or another resorted to various ruses when leaving a child with a baby-sitter to avoid the desperate clinging and pleading for the parent not to leave. The child is protesting the departure because when the parent leaves the departure seems to him permanent. Young children can't be reasonable about specific calendar or clock time which adults take for granted. An hour, a week, a month—it's all the same, it's *absence*. The absence of a parent can be felt by the child as abandonment and arouse fear or anger. Prolonged absence can sometimes be construed as death.

When five-year-old Natasha's father returned home from the war after more than a year's absence, Natasha would not call him "Papa." Her papa had *gone*. This was a stranger in his place. And although Natasha soon grew to love her father and developed a close relationship with him, she was, for many years, unable to call him "Papa."

Similarly, six-year-old Alice, who knew that her father although living was hospitalized indefinitely and unable to communicate, persisted in telling people that her father was dead.

After working for many years with preschool and young school-age children, I recognize how trying separation can be for some children, how it can sap a child's attention. To alleviate the distress I always looked for concrete, realistic assurances. When a nursery-school child was having a difficult initial adjustment, I advised taking an item from mommy's handbag to keep till she returns, or perhaps making a phone call home. I also made sure that a mother's *promise* to return at a particular functional, not clock, time was kept. To minimize children's concern or apprehension about separation, I encouraged parents of camp and boarding-school children to maintain (or cultivate, if necessary) simple, direct, but *frequent* communication by means of letters, small packages, calls. Elaborate or expensive items don't necessarily convey caring to the child. I still remember Linda who while she was in boarding school received from her father an enormous glittering package on her seventh birthday. There were ribbons around each item, and Linda chose to play with all the ribbons for a long time, ignoring the numerous presents, which apparently overwhelmed her and did not seem to represent her father whom she had not seen for several months.

Experience in separation from important objects or temporary separation from friendly adults and family members helps the gradually maturing child to gain concepts of dependence and independence. In such experiences a child may overcome the feeling of loss by finding temporary substitutes for those he or she misses. Children may thus gain trust in forming new relationships. All of this contributes to children's understanding and to their mental health, adding to their strength for coping with death and separation.

Another area of children's experience that has bearing on death is knowledge of basic causes and of practical prevention of death.

One of the first questions that the nursery-school children asked when they learned that Rachel had died (chapter 2) had to do with causes of death. Although they cannot understand scientific explanations, modern children are personally acquainted with medical prevention of dangerous diseases through inoculations. Parents confronted with the unpleasant chore of taking children to get their shots* might clarify that care is being taken to *protect* children, that the shots do actually prevent disease. There is the realistic assurance of not getting the particular disease or dying from it.

Since accidents constitute a major cause of death in the United States, especially among children, parents

---

*It is unfortunate, I think, that the common English word for injection should be such a violent and scary word as "shot."

and teachers alike can learn with young children practical prevention of accidents. Certainly, American children are well acquainted with cars and car accidents as well as with traffic laws and safety measures designed to prevent car accidents and death. Children as young as two and three already have some knowledge of cars, and slightly older children recognize "a wrong way of driving." Here adult responsibility for practical, consistent indoctrination about safety and adult practice of accident prevention are entirely appropriate. Such a procedure would give children a realistic concept of the prevention of accidental premature death.

Knowledge of some causes and personal prevention of death are of immediate concern to children. Four-year-old Wayne, learning (from TV) that smoking may cause cancer and cancer is a dangerous disease, became adamant that his mother stop smoking. She didn't take him seriously at first; then, to avoid his vehement protest she didn't smoke in her child's presence. However, he was apt to catch her at it. Finally, Wayne pressured his mother into giving up smoking entirely. It was both a rational as well as an emotional act on the child's part. Wayne wanted assurance that his mother wasn't going to die. at least not of cancer caused by smoking!

Thus, working with children on prevention of disease and death in accordance with established scientific findings does not mean avoiding *inevitable* death or overlooking its occurrence and consequences. Rather, practical education in prevention means cultivating a strong regard for healthy living and doing something to promote a longer life for oneself and for others.

Although the taboo against professional and popular teaching and discussion about death (as well as against bringing the subject up with children) had existed for many decades, the last decade brought a tremendous change. Along with an increase in research reports and the publication of studies on death in professional journals and in educational periodicals, numerous articles have also appeared in various popular magazines and in mass-appeal TV programs. *Business Week* is a publication one would not at all expect to be concerned with death education. Yet, the April 5, 1976, issue has in its Personal Business Supplement an article entitled "Coping with Death in the Family," that is indeed concerned with death education, covering fully psychological, legal, and practical aspects.

> The dramatic news today is that there are experts on death and dying and a large and growing body of knowledge about the subject. Thanks to the work of such people as Chicago psychiatrist-author Dr. Elisabeth Kübler-Ross, the burden of coping wth death—from the shock of learning that a spouse or a child is terminally ill, through the death, funeral, and subsequent adjustment period—is being lightened for many families. "There's a healthier, more open attitude today toward death and how to handle it," says Dr. Austin H. Kutscher, who teaches a new course called thanatology (the study of death) at the Columbia University medical school. "People are getting help they couldn't have gotten two or three years ago."[7]

The article focuses on the wisdom of honest explanations of death to children and of encouraging their participation in funerals. Outstanding authorities in the

7. "Coping with Death in the Family," *Business Week,* April 5, 1976, p. 93.

field of thanatology are cited, especially Elisabeth Kübler-Ross and her book *On Death and Dying.*

Programs on death education are being announced and attended in communities throughout the country. In the summer of 1976, a child guidance center on Long Island, New York, offered a program on "Coping with death for mothers of families in which there has been a recent death . . . to concentrate on helping mothers and their children to cope with the loss." In Chicago, under the auspices of the Psychoanalytic Institute a "New Center to Help Young Cope with Death" opened in December of 1976.

Recognizing the fact that children seldom have an opportunity to see the dead or to ask questions, and are growing up in ignorance and with misconceptions about death, death has recently become a proper subject for childhood education. There are now fifteen hundred public schools which engage in the study of death.[8] One elementary school in Florida has a program of "adopting a grandparent" from a nearby nursing home by a class of seven- to eight-year-olds.[9] The program includes visits and other communication by the children on an informal but regular basis. In one instance when the "adopted grandmother" died, the children expressed sadness, talked about it, and wrote a condolence letter to the family. The experience proved to be of special help to one of the children whose father later died. It also prepared the children to be more understanding with another "grandmother" who was dying.

8. Hannelore Wass and Judith Shaak, "Helping Children Understand Death through Literature," *Childhood Education,* November–December 1976.

9. Esstoya Whitney, "Grandma—She Died," *Childhood Education,* November–December 1976.

Judging by the evident trend of having courses on death offered in colleges, in adult education programs, and in high schools and public schools, the still uncommon term, "thanatology," may soon become a household word.

One might well ask whether in a country technologically and educationally less advanced than ours there are also taboos and ways of escaping the reality of death, and whether there are (similar to our) trends of accelerated death education. The answer would involve a historical and anthropological study beyond the scope of this book. However, ordinary tourist travel to geographically neighboring Mexico will give us at least a glimpse of traditions and prevalent attitudes toward death that are different from ours.

There is a national holiday in Mexico, called El Día de los Muertos (The Day of the Dead).[10] Although November 2 is the official date of the holiday, it is too important a day to start and end by prescribed calendar. There are preliminary days as well as days following the holiday. On the Day of the Dead, the Mexicans believe, the souls return to earth. This is a festive occasion! The cemeteries are bedecked with traditional floral displays (artificial flowers are also acceptable), and paths to the graves are strewn with petals, so the dead will find their way. Bowls and baskets of special foods (according to the region) are placed for them at the cemetery or at home to show the dead a warm welcome! New pottery is made for the holiday, and there are special censers and candlesticks made of black-glazed clay adorned with

10. Frances Toor, *A Treasury of Mexican Folk Ways* (New York: Crown, 1947).

angels, birds, or flowers. As befits a festivity in Mexico, there is music and dancing and in some places an exciting display of fireworks. It is a religious holiday with pre-Christian and Christian aspects, but with equally important folklore about the requirements of the dead, and with feasting and celebrations for the living.

Since there is no celebration in Mexico in which children do not take part, the Day of the Dead has many attractions for them. There is an abundance of special sweets and toys in the shape of the symbols of death: skulls, skeletons, coffins. Everyone asserts that these shapes are not scary to Mexican children. It's a pleasure and fun to bite into a candy skull! A popular toy consists of a cardboard coffin from which a skeleton jumps out when a string is pulled, "which delights the children."[11]

Although there is unmistakable respect for the dead in this Mexican holiday, there is also evident whimsey and humor about their "return" and there is the enjoyment of family and community celebration in honor of the dead. Above all, there appears to be no fear, and no rejection or denial of death. Does humor facilitate the removal of fear and anxiety or even the acceptance of the reality of death?

In the study *Children and the Death of a President* several jokes were told by older children after the tragedy. One joke was: "What did Caroline get for her birthday? She got a Jack-in-the-box."[12]

The well-known folklorists, I. and P. Opie, writing about the folklore of British schoolchildren, cite humorous verses about death. Among them is a mock lament:

11. Ibid., p. 57.
12. Wolfenstein and Kliman, eds., *Children and the Death of a President,* p. 75.

Little Willie's dead,
Jam him in the coffin,
For you don't get the chance
Of a funeral of'en.[13]

Perhaps the reader too may be familiar with blithe childhood rhymes about death.

There is humor about death also in adult folklore, as seen in some tombstone verses. A stone located in Skaneateles, New York, has the following:

Underneath this pile of stones.
Lies all that's left of Sally Jones.
Her name was Lord, it was not Jones.
But Jones was used to rhyme with stones.[14]

And one in Ithaca, New York, is inscribed in the first person:

While on earth, my knee was lame,
I had to nurse and heed it.
But now I'm in a better place
Where I don't even need it.

While humor may serve as a release of tension and as superficial escape from sorrow, humankind has always sought the more profound and spiritual means afforded by religion to deal with death.

Every religion prescribes for its adherents regard for the dead, rules for burial and the funeral, regulations

13. I. and P. Opie, *The Lore and Language of School Children,* quoted in Anthony, *The Discovery of Death in Childhood and After,* p. 76.
14. From a display of "American Gravestone Art, 1647–1903," sponsored by the Ohio Foundation for the Arts, and collected by Francis and Ivan Rigby of Brooklyn, N.Y., for exhibit in 1976.

for family mourning and memorializing. For faithful adherents, a religious prescription gives guidance at a time of disabling distress, and religious belief brings solace to a troubled mind. We assume, of course, that religious adults share their beliefs and feelings with children and that they too benefit from religion in coping with death.

Since we have frequently referred to psychiatric and psychological authorities for helping children cope with death, it would be of interest to consider the relative wisdom of religion and psychiatry. This topic is intelligently discussed in an essay by Audrey Gordon.

> Judaism does not permit the mourner to escape the reality of death; it bids him see it, and then it leads him through a whole network of burial and mourning procedures whose purpose is to help him come to terms with it. In doing this it is in harmony with psychiatric literature, which abounds with examples of the fearful consequences of death-denial and repression of grief. The Talmudic sages centuries ago seem to have sensed the same truth that psychiatrists now articulate, which is that "the recognition of death is a necessity for continuing life, and grief is a necessary and unavoidable process in normative psychological functioning."[15]

Although the above discussion refers to only one religion, other religions must have *their* wisdom for meeting physical and spiritual needs in time of death, offering strength for the bereaved living, and special consideration for the dead. It would not be within our province now to compare different religions. The

15. Audrey Gordon, "The Psychological Wisdom of the Law," in Jack Riemer, ed., *Jewish Reflections on Death* (New York: Schocken Books, 1974), p. 97.

reader must consider this topic in the light of his or her own religion or nonreligion, his or her social and spiritual values.

A discussion of religion, specifically God Himself, in children's experience with death occurs in a unique book of fiction by John B. Coburn.[16] Written by a Christian minister, the story is told in the first person by eleven-year-old Dan whose much-loved baby sister dies, followed soon afterward by his dog, Bonnie. The author portrays in casual and amusing fashion a familiar type of family—the rivalry between the two brothers and their dislike for doing chores, the bossiness of the older sister, and the darling youngest, Anne.

When Anne dies, Dan asks: "Dad, why did God kill her?" The answer he receives is: "That's a good question, son. A good question."[17] Dan continues asking brief questions about God's responsibility throughout the attention to Anne's funeral, the selection and the singing of hymns during church service, and his experiences with helpful, caring relatives and friends. No dogmatic answers are given by the father or mother, but answers and further questions come from every member of the family. Dan struggles to accept the absence of Anne's body after cremation and the disposal of the ashes. He questions his father about "where" Anne is, since she isn't in her body.

"The simplest way to put it, I guess, is to say she's with God." The implication of the story is that it is human to question and seek God in trying to understand the tangible, visible, sometimes painful events in

16. John B. Coburn, *Anne and the Sand Dobbies: A Story about Death for Children and Their Parents* (New York: Seabury Press, 1964).
17. Ibid., p. 55.

life, as well as the existing invisibles—the "sand dob-bies," or the spirit of a person no longer in the body, or a heaven. The story provokes thinking and discussion about both the reality and the mystery of the religious aspect of death.

Also in the realm of the spiritual, but not as abstract as religious concepts, are artistic expressions as reactions to encounters with death.

Five-year-old Helen, a musically responsive child who was noticeably distressed about the death of the chicks in school (chapter 4) had spontaneously com-posed what one might well call a dirge. It consisted of a doleful tune with rhythmic wails, and, though the lyrics were difficult to record, the refrain of "oh, so sad, our chick is dead" was quite clear. The singing extended itself to a slow dance. Other children joined Helen in the funereal movement and humming. The twenty-minute performance had the impressive mood and feeling of a dirge. Children, younger and older ones, will respond to the beauty of special sad music—a dirge, a funeral march, a song about death. When adults appreciate the music themselves they are able to share their impression with children without dwelling on despair. "Go Tell Aunt Rhodie," a folk song, is very popular with pre-school children—even if occasionally a child may be moved to tears.

Go tell Aunt Rhodie / Go tell Aunt Rhodie
Go tell Aunt Rhodie the old grey goose is dead.
The gander is weeping / The gander is weeping
The gander is weeping because his wife is dead.
The goslings are crying / The goslings are crying.
The goslings are crying because their mother's dead.
She died last Friday / She died last Friday
She died last Friday standing on her head.

Coming to the last verse with its change of focus, children find relief and a welcome measure of mirth. They seem to enjoy the tension and drama of the "grey goose is dead" trauma, and the release of tension in the absurd condition of "standing on her head." Thus the song seems to serve as aesthetic acquaintance with the sadness caused by death.

The same would be true of some poetic composition, as in the rhythm and mood of the following:

On a green, green hill / I saw two rabbits come.
One he was a piper; / the other played a drum,
on a green, green hill in the morning.

A hunter shot the drummer; / the drummer lost his life.
The other little rabbit / now sadly plays his fife
on a green, green hill in the morning.[18]

Rose Mukerji describes how a class of six-year-olds reacted through movement to the news of the death of Martin Luther King, Jr. With dramatic gestures and pantomime they strove to express their knowledge and horror and sadness for which they had no words.[19]

Music and body movement are often the most available means for individual and group expression in school or at home, but other art mediums may be available and suitable for particular children, especially the medium of drawing and painting. The beautiful picture that Mark-O (in *The Magic Moth*) made required all his creative energies; it eased his tragic encounter with death and it expressed aesthetically a spirit that was shared by his family.

18. *It's Raining Said John Twaining,* in *Danish Nursery Rhymes,* trans. and illus. N. M. Bodecker (New York: Atheneum, 1973).
19. Rose Mukerji, "When Words Fail," *Childhood Education,* April 1970.

Although "words" do often "fail," writing for older children or dictating for younger ones can serve as an effective means of expression and for sharing thoughts and feelings. In the study of children's reaction to the death of President Kennedy (chapter 6), the researchers had observed that opportunity for writing essays or reports proved that children were noticeably more articulate and creative with the written, as opposed to the spoken, word.[20] Written composition appeals to many children and provides a means for significant expression. Sometimes simple letters provide such expression. They may be condolence letters, mentioned earlier, meant to convey sympathy, or they may be letters about the death of a person or a pet. A nine-year-old, sending a valentine to his grandmother, saw fit in the same letter to tell about the death of a pet:

> My lizard died of a cold. She looked like a little green jewel when she died. She died since the heat was too low.
> Love, Danny.

How typically childlike it is to tell so much in a few simple words: concern for the cause of death with implication of regret (yet no complaint about the "low heat"), and an expression of poetic appreciation—"a little green jewel." Yes, given an opportunity and responsive adults, children in a few apt words articulate a basic concept.

"There is always a starting, and there is always an ending."

In the course of living with children, while teaching, parenting, working with, or simply befriending them at

20. Wolfenstein and Kliman, eds., *Children and the Death of a President.*

various ages and levels, we are bound to encounter death. The death may be regarded as unreconcilable tragedy or resented as an act of intrusion in the activities of the living, or it may cause feelings of helplessness and fear in adults as well as children. However, taking into account children's understanding and feelings appropriate to their ages, adults can help children (and themselves) by clarifying experiences of separation, by offering religious or spiritual explanations, and by using artistic means for expression or release of ideas and feelings about death. Thus, through death one may acquire a deeper knowledge of life and of living.

ADDITIONAL BIBLIOGRAPHY

Becker, Earnest. *The Denial of Death.* New York: The Free Press, 1973. A psychological study considering the protection of denial, and the need for recognition of death and sorrow.

De Bruyn, M. G. *The Beaver Who Wouldn't Die.* Chicago: Follett Publishing Company, 1975. Children's book. When his wish to live forever comes true, is the beaver happy? Well, not exactly.

Galen, Harlene. "A Matter of Life and Death." *Young Children,* August 1972. Practical and insightful guidance for preschool teachers about the subject of death and its use as a vital area of curriculum. Good "References."

Goleman, Daniel. "The Child Will Always Be There: Real Love Doesn't Die." *Psychology Today,* September 1976. An interview with psychiatrist Elisabeth Kübler-Ross about "the sudden death of children, the anguish of parents, and how the dying teach us to live."

Gordon, David Cole. *Overcoming the Fear of Death.* New York: Macmillan Publishing Co., 1970. A study of the fears and anxieties pertaining to death, and related loss of self.

Kastenbaum, Robert. "We Covered Death Today." *Death Education,** Spring 1977. A broad critique of social trends and the nature of death education programs and practices.

Kolls, Mardel. "Reflection on My Children Experiencing Death." *Death Education,* Summer 1977. Confrontations with death on different occasions and on children's own level; the benefits of direct experience and of sharing feelings.

Koocher, Gerald P. "Why Isn't the Gerbil Moving Any More?" *Children Today,* January 1975. When children's questions concerning death go unanswered, or even unasked, mental health problems occur. Helpful suggestions to parents and teachers.

Langdone, John. *Death Is a Noun.* 4th printing. Boston: Little, Brown & Company, 1972. Lively presentation with a historical perspective of psychological, legal, religious, moral, and other aspects of death, including discussion of euthanasia and capital punishment.

McDonald, Marjorie. "Helping Children to Understand Death: An Experience with Death in a Nursery School." *Journal of Nursery Education,*† November 1963. The author, a psychiatrist, explains how teachers and parents in one school helped children face the death of Wendy's mother—the facts, and their own feelings.

Meathenia, Peggy Sue. "An Experience with Fear in the Lives of Children." *Childhood Education,* November 1971. A kindergarten teacher utilizes the dramatization of stories to help children express their fear and over-

---

*Published by Hemisphere Publishing Corp., 1025 Vermont Ave., N.W., Washington, D.C. 20005.

†The journal is now called *Young Children.*

come the trauma of a devastating, death-causing tornado in their area (Lubbock, Texas).

Moody, Raymond A. *Life after Life.* Paperback. New York: Bantam Books, Inc., 1975. A strange but medically valid account of firsthand experiences during and following clinical death of a few minutes duration.

Parness, Estelle. "Effects of Experiences with Loss and Death among Preschool Children." *Children Today,* November–December 1975. Concise and clear account of children's stressful behavior caused by loss or significant separation; teachers' and parents' helpful attitudes and actions.

Peck, Robert Newton. *A Day No Pigs Would Die,* Paperback. New York: Dell Publishing Co., 1974. An acclaimed short novel about a Shaker family in Vermont. Portrays the strength of a father's influence on a boy, and the boy's deep struggle to accept death's inevitability and consequences.

Self, Margaret C. *Come Away!* Cranbury, N.J.: A. S. Barnes & Co., Inc., 1948. An absorbing realistic novel (out of print) about a strong, highly imaginative child; his successful caring for and deep devotion to a horse; and his profound experience of losing the horse.

Sharapan, Hedda. "Mister Rogers' Neighborhood: Dealing with Death on a Children's Television Series." *Death Education,* Spring 1977. A psychological review of a TV program's content and its beneficial effect on children and parents.

Skorpen, Liesel Moak. *Old Arthur.* New York: Harper & Row, Publishers, Inc., 1972. A children's book about an old dog who requires special care and love, and is getting both from a child.

West, Jessamyn. *The Woman Said Yes.* New York: Harcourt Brace Jovanovich, Inc., 1976. An autobiographical narrative involving three related women, each possessing a powerfully assertive spirit and a will to make life worthwhile; includes a positive decision to terminate life when it is reduced to mere pain.

Wolf, Anna W. M., ed. *Helping Your Child to Understand Death.* Child Study Association of America, 1958. A comprehensive, down-to-earth booklet, answering actual parents' questions on facing death situations with children.

INDEX